IN SAFE HANDS

Published by

abz Publications

8 Abbey Close, St Johns

Worcester

WR2 4HR

© Colin J Abbott & Debra A Abbott 2012

A CIP catalogue record for this book is available from
the British Library.

ISBN 978-0-9572151-0-8

Printed and bound in Great Britain by Jellyfish
Solutions, Southampton, Hampshire.

IN SAFE HANDS

NIGEL SIMS'
FOOTBALL MEMORIES

Colin J Abbott & Debra A Abbott

Foreword by Charlie Aitken

abz Publications

To Nathan
Best wishes
CA

Dedicated to the memory of my younger brother
Paul Stephen Abbott
1968-2008

Nigel and Marjorie Sims would like to take this opportunity to thank, Consultant Orthopaedic Surgeon Mr E.T.R. James of the Morriston Hospital, Swansea, for his work and assistance, past and future for keeping Aston Villa's greatest post-war 'keeper alive and kicking!

Contents

Acorns Children's Hospice

Acorns Children's Hospice currently cares for over 600 children as well as providing support for their families at every stage of their child's life and into bereavement.

Acorns provides short break, emergency and end-of-life care from the hospices, with a dedicated community team to support the family 24 hours a day, 365 days a year.

Acorns have three ten-bed children's hospices: Acorns in Birmingham (located in Selly Oak), Acorns in the Black Country (located in Walsall) and Acorns for the Three Counties (located in Worcester). The hospices are designed to be a home-from-home to help children enjoy their stay and make the most of every day.

With hospice running costs of over £8million a year, Acorns relies heavily on the community to fund the majority of its activities. From every £1 you give 88p is spent on providing the vital care and support that our children and families rely on. There is no charge to families for using the services we provide.

We urgently need your support to help us continue to provide our specialist care services. **NOW is the time** to support your local children's hospice.

To find out how you can support the **NOW is the time** campaign. Visit **www.acorns.org.uk** email **info@acorns.org.uk** or call **01564 825000**

Foreword
By
Charlie Aitken

Some time ago I was approached by Colin Abbott and his wife Debra and asked if I would be willing to put a foreword together, for a book they were writing, about a former teammate of mine at Aston Villa, goalkeeper Nigel Sims.

I was delighted and honoured when asked, and so I put together a few words and anecdotes that I thought might be interesting and raise a couple of smiles.

It was 1959 when I joined Aston Villa; I arrived at Villa Park straight from school in Edinburgh. I was amazed when I discovered there were nearly fifty professionals on the books and they fielded four professional teams, as well as the Senior and Reserve sides. Like most clubs, Villa had a third team playing in the Midland Intermediate League and the fourth team played in the Warwickshire Football Combination.

I was in awe of many of the senior pros, but one who stood out for me was Nigel Sims, the first team goalkeeper. He was a huge personality and the lads looked up to him, especially for someone like me playing in the fourth team at the time. It wasn't just his ability, but the all-round contribution to the playing staff and his general banter.

For a goalkeeper Nigel was huge and he had this amazing flexibility, which he worked on every day. His training was separate from the other players and, well Nigel had a way of sorting those extra pounds if they managed to creep on, he had a plastic suit. I'll never forget the first time he wore it in training. It was amazing and amusing at the same time. Nigel did his training session in it, but then after training he was there emptying this suit which was like a bucketful of sweat, it was a great success.

When I managed to play in the first team alongside Nigel, it didn't take me long to find out that he didn't take any prisoners coming for the ball. It didn't make any difference who it was, whether it was an opponent or a member of his own team.

I remember Peter McParland telling me, when he played against him for Ireland, that Nigel nearly knocked him unconscious coming for the ball. This was when Nigel was representing the Football League. Then one day on the pitch during a Manchester United game, Nigel saved a Bobby Charlton shot and took 'the mick' saying, "My missus could have hit it harder than that," he said it so Bobby could hear 'the crack' made at his expense.

In training and at all times Nigel took it personally. If he was ever beaten by a shot he would respond with, "I could have chucked my cap on that!" I have to say, it was an all-round honour to play with Nigel, in all aspects of the games and I wish him many more years of health and happiness.

Charlie Aitken

A WORD FROM SIR DOUG ELLIS

It gives me great pleasure to be asked to contribute to the biography of one of Aston Villa's most respected servants. I saw many players come and go in my thirty years as Chairman of this fine club. As I remember, Nigel was a modest man and a model professional. On only one occasion did I feel the need to have a word with Nigel and that was when I suspected his weight was increasing slightly.

I joined the Villa board in December 1968 and before that I served my time on the terraces as a fan of the club. It's fair to say that Nigel was held in very high esteem by the fans and many from my generation would say that Nigel Sims remains to this day one of Aston Villa's most prominent post-war goalkeepers.

Sir Doug Ellis PRESIDENT EMERITUS

AUTHOR'S NOTES

I was pulled kicking and screaming into the early sixties to take my place in the fourth generation of a Midland-based family of Aston Villa supporters. Whilst toddling around I learned my ABCs and 123s - but for me the names of Villa's legends such as Archie Hunter, Billy Walker and Howard Spencer were as commonplace as Muffin the Mule and they probably had a kick to equal the four-legged beast. My Granddad's favourite player was Tom 'Pongo' Waring and I vividly remember my Dad's was the goalkeeper Nigel Sims - who many Villa supporters have said was the clubs best post-war 'keeper. By the time I was four-years-old I could recite the 1957 Cup Final team that had been victorious only seven years before I was born. Little did I know that half a century later they would still be the last victorious Villa team. In 1972 I saw my first live match and I was hooked, but why wouldn't I be, it was in the blood. To this day I still struggle to see how opposition fans can get so excited after scoring against Aston Villa, the Villa aren't just a football team, they are an institution and I feel honoured to be able to call myself a supporter.

In 2008 I had the opportunity to meet Nigel Sims; over the years I had listened to so many conversations about the chap that I felt like I already knew him. This was quite a surreal experience and I soon realised that even in his later years he hadn't lost any of his imposing presence or stature and he had a giant personality to match. The idea to write a book on the Villa had been simmering for a long time. Friends would ask a question regarding Aston Villa and the floodgates would open; hours later they would say, "You should put all this down in writing." Meeting my wife pushed me further towards this idea and with her writing experience, albeit writing for pleasure, and Nigel's seal of approval, I thought I would give it my best shot and write his biography, so here it is. If you enjoy reading this half as much as I did listening to his stories and anecdotes then you should not be disappointed.

Thanks and Acknowledgements

I would like to extend my grateful thanks to the following friends and associates, who made this book possible. My thanks come in no particular order and I hope that I have remembered and acknowledged you all. My sincere apologies if I have overlooked anyone.

My initial thanks go to my wife, she has had to live, breathe and sleep Aston Villa for longer than any good wife should (so she says). Debra, you made this book possible, Y.M.L.Y.H.

Huge thanks go to Nigel & Marjorie, who have become personal friends, and for agreeing to my writing his story. I have enjoyed every moment. Thank you both.

To former teammates, their spouses and associates of Nigel's, who were generous, helpful and willingly gave me their time and use of personal albums, scrapbooks and photographs:

Aston Villa

Charlie Aitken, Villa's record appearance holder, (660) for agreeing to do the foreword.

Sir Doug Ellis.

Stan Crowther, Jackie Sewell, Jimmy MacEwan, Alan Deakin, Ron & Shirley Wylie, Gordon Lee, Alan O'Neill and Harry Burrows.

Wolves

Malcolm Finlayson and Johnny Walker.

Peterborough United

Peter Deakin and Peter McNamee.

Toronto City

Tony Book.

John Lerwill who assisted and listened patiently to so many questions. Norman Crandles for the Canadian information.

I would like to thank Norman Hood for kindly supplying an amazing one off caricature for publication and Neville Evans for his assistance with Nigel's memorabilia. Many thanks go to Gerry Hitchens' family for use of their personal photographs and Simon Goodyear, an author, who has given me invaluable advice. My thanks go to the family of Arthur Sabin for allowing me access to their private album of Arthur and to Barry Swash, of South Staffs Football Programmes for various photographs.

I extend my thanks to Paul Faulkner, Aston Villa Football Club Chief Executive. Laura Brett, Aston Villa Football Club Archivist. Rob Bishop, Aston Villa Football Club Programme Editor and John Greenfield/Alan Williams, Aston Villa Football Club Commercial Department, who have provided invaluable assistance with this project.

Thanks to Peter Lane, official Peterborough United Historian, who was very helpful and patient with my calls. A special mention also to his wife Sandee.

My continued thanks to Peterborough City Council Mayor.

Ian Cook, Arsenal Football Club Historian.

John Hendley, Wolverhampton Wanderers Programme Editor.

A special and personal thanks to everyone at Acorns Children's Hospice for their amazing work and dedication, helping to enrich the lives of so many.

Thanks to my brother Geoff for continued support and nephew Jay Abbott, for the website design and management.

Grateful thanks to Colorsport Images, for Nigel Sims photographs used in this publication.
Good friends:
Thank you Jon Farrelly for the unlimited use of his cherished 'Villa News & Record' bound volumes and photographs and for

trusting me with them. To Karl Court, for his assistance in my endless pursuit of ex-Villa players. Martin 'Mozza' Moss and Andy 'Turnstile' Ullah, for supplying everything else!

'Mr Fanzine' Dave Woodhall, and to Nigel Stanton, who came up with the title 'In Safe Hands.' Nice one Nige!

Ade, Hedda and the rest of the 'Cherry Tree Crew' for bouncing around all the ideas and providing some invaluable feedback.

Thanks to Mark Clarey, my driver, a Villa convert, and friend for over twenty-seven years. Neil Alderson, a librarian extraordinaire, for his proofreading capabilities (along with sidekick Richard Bourne); luckily Neil had access to all the books required on punctuation! Richard Leach for some great research and Bill Howell for the much-needed contacts.

Marc Taylor for his sterling work with the camera.

Last, but certainly not least are three lads who I happened luckily to stumble upon, who will be the reason for this project succeeding.

Dave Clarke, a good friend and a true football fanatic, if ever there was one, who gave me some very important leads and ideas.

Andy Vaughan, owner of Wigan based Vaughan Media. **www.vaughanmedia.co.uk**

Andy Greenhalgh who was responsible for the fantastic cover design. **www.aggd.co.uk**

My thanks to my sons, Bradley, Tom and daughter Tilly, for all the fetching and carrying. To my son Kyle, who has always been my sounding board, listening to me patiently whenever we have talked and lastly my great-grandfather, grandfather and father who made sure I followed in the family footsteps, and were responsible for my love of the Claret and Blue side of Birmingham! Thank the lord.

PROLOGUE

May 4th 1957 was not a particularly relevant or memorable day for the majority of people, but a magnificent day in the lives of supporters, players and everybody else associated with Aston Villa Football Club. This was their date with destiny, the 1957 FA Cup Final, beneath the white twin towers of the legendary Wembley Stadium. The famous Midlands side plying their wits against Matt Busby's newly-crowned Champions of English football, and seemingly unbeatable, Manchester United. Very few football fans outside Birmingham would have thought these chaps from 'Brum' had a cat in hell's chance of holding aloft the FA Cup and bringing the famous trophy back to Villa Park.

In the season of 1948/49, seventeen-year-old David Nigel Sims took an apprenticeship at Wolverhampton Wanderers Football Club and, ten months after signing for the team, he was given his first taste of success, following an injury to the first team 'keeper Bert Williams. Nigel played three consecutive matches in the following six days and hoped that his unbeaten match record would be enough to secure a first team place for the forthcoming Wembley showcase FA Cup Final against Leicester City the following Saturday. But for Nigel this was not his time and Williams recovered from his latest injury ready to take his place in the starting XI.

Nigel continued the best part of a decade with Wolves but only saw a total of a thirty-nine first team appearances. But in March '56 Aston Villa manager, Eric Houghton came knocking and he signed for the Villa where his fortunes and the club's would soon change for the better.

The Villa management had been busy bolstering the side since the shock departure of two of its international players, Danny Blanchflower, defecting to White Hart Lane in October '54 and Tommy Thompson. After watching the Irishman's progress at his new club Tottenham, Thompson decided he wanted pastures new and after insisting on a transfer was on his way to the north-west to join Preston North End.

Only half a century before this the major players of the day were honoured to be signed or even linked to the Midlands giants - it was unheard of that players requested to leave Villa Park.

Aston Villa responded quickly. First to be signed was Pat Saward from Division Three South side Millwall. The Republic of Ireland wing-half had been getting rave reviews down at Cold Blow Lane, though he had been playing against far inferior opposition than he would come up against in the top-flight. His signing wasn't sufficient to quell the fans' unrest and this was to be appeased by bringing in the renowned goalscorer from Everton, Dave Hickson, in the September. But this wasn't to be the club's salvation and Hickson was gone two months later to Huddersfield Town, after only finding the back of the net once in a dozen starts for the Villa. He in turn was replaced by another big name, in the shape of Jackie Sewell. This was the man who only four years earlier had commanded England's largest transfer fee when he had departed Notts County for Sheffield Wednesday for the then staggering price of £34,500.

Aston Villa were showing the football world that they meant business and were going to awaken what everyone was calling: 'The sleeping giant of English football!'

Other signings who would ultimately play in the final of '57 alongside Sewell were being targeted. In February 1956, came centre-half Jimmy Dugdale from rivals West Bromwich Albion, whom he had starred for in their 1954 FA Cup Final victory. Leslie Smith was bought in the same month from Wolverhampton Wanderers, to be followed only weeks later by his former Molineux teammate Nigel Sims.

In the May of the following year, Villa history would be written and Nigel would play a key part with the rest of the newly-assembled squad. The game - the 1957 FA Cup Final, the opposition - the seemingly unstoppable Manchester United, the venue - Wembley Stadium. This game carried such expectations; if the Villa claimed the day they would make history in being the first team to win the FA Cup for a record seven times. A win for Manchester United would see them secure the 'double', just as their 'Claret and Blue' opponents had back in the early football days of 1897. Villa had managed to defend their double title history against League Champions Newcastle United in the 1905 FA Cup Final, and eight years later they were back at Crystal Palace to claim victory over northern giants of the time, Sunderland.

Would this newly-formed side be able to take victory again and see Nigel and the '57 team secure a legendary place in Villa folklore?

CHAPTER ONE

THEN THERE WERE THREE

On August 9th 1931 David Nigel Sims was born, the third and last son to Jack and Edith Sims, in a small and idyllic village called Coton-in-the-Elms, eight miles south of Burton-on-Trent. Coton was a mining village at the time and had a modest population of six-hundred people. Like most small villages, it was a friendly place where everybody knew everyone and had time for each other. Jack Junior and George were the first two sons and they had a simple and happy early life in the rural Derbyshire countryside. This would also be the case for David, the new family addition.

Cradley Pit was the local colliery and a leading employer in the district. Jack Senior grafted each day making sure the mine tunnels were the right size and then laying the coal cart tracks in them, Edith, like most miners' wives, stayed at home to keep house and raise Jack, George and David - who was now known by his middle name Nigel. "Mother realised early on that as I grew up my name was probably going to be shortened to Dave and she didn't like the idea of that, so it was dropped. Had Mother known that in future when I joined the Villa I would be nicknamed 'Nigger' she would probably have settled for Dave. In those days most of the players would have some kind of nickname that was related to their surname. Peter McParland was known as 'Packy.' They really were just names, totally harmless and no malice intended in any way. My nickname certainly didn't carry the ramifications it would today but times have changed."

Soon enough Nigel began school and this meant a five-mile bike ride with George to Swadlincote where they attended Gresley School. This regular cycling would go a long way to strengthen Nigel's upper legs and thighs and shape his future physique. He excelled in all sports the school had to offer and even at primary school age he was starting to develop into a handy little footballer. As well as kicking the football about, he also had a passion for cricket - where he proved to be more than a demon fast bowler; much to the envy of the other schools Gresley came up against. His earliest recollections of football were of being put up front; he played in this position for the school team and Coton Village Junior Team. His size was an advantage and made Nigel a formidable centre-forward. Most kids his age didn't fancy the idea of taking the ball off him, but he also had versatility and if the team played against another local village side with a dazzling winger ready to put a few crosses into the penalty area, the coach could reshuffle the line-up and Nigel would be made to play at right-back, with the instructions ringing in his ears, "Put the ball and the man into touch." Nigel wasn't the only footballer in the family as older brother Jack played centre-half for the village seniors. One day the senior team's goalkeeper didn't turn up, so Jack used a very persuasive manner when asking a young twelve-year-old Nigel to go in goal. Nigel remembers how he "got involved," and managed to get down sharpish and at full stretch was able to push the ball around the right-hand upright and deny his opponents what looked to be a certain goal. The lads couldn't believe it. This was a team of blokes and here was a twelve-year-old kid pulling off saves that their regular 'keeper could only dream about. Nigel remained in goal for the Coton Swifts from that day on, though he had no say in the matter. To this day he remembers that first village seniors' save as the most memorable one he ever made. Meanwhile Jack's reputation as a cracking centre-half for Coton was spreading. It wasn't too long before he was spotted and the Birmingham City scout came knocking on the Sims' front door. An offer was put to Jack, but he didn't want to know and the 'Blues' scout went away empty-handed. Young Nigel looked on: By now he was passionate about the game and desperately wanted to be a footballer. He sat and watched his brother throw away the chance of a lifetime, "It would have meant everything to have had that football scout knocking at the door for me and not our Jack!" He was well and truly hooked and whenever he could he would call on his mates to come out for a game of footie; but he wasn't interested in the conventional five or eleven-a-side games. He just wanted them to take turns shooting at his goal to see how many he could save, or he would assign a few of the lads to mark him while the rest would take it in turns to float the ball over and he would try to catch the crosses as they came.

The lads continued to play summer footie out in the fields, as the season turned to autumn and then the worst village winter on record. The high snow cut Coton off from the outside world for weeks, but this wasn't enough to hold back one determined young 'keeper. Nigel would sit on the floorboards in his room, with his back against one wall, throwing a tennis ball against the other for hour after hour, taking turns to catch it with each hand. When he tired of that he would throw the ball with more force and at different angles so he would have to anticipate which way it would come back.

When Nigel wasn't honing his footballing skills, he was out in the local orchards scrumping a pullover full of apples, or he would spend time in Catton and Croxall Woods climbing the trees with the other lads. If the fancy took, they would venture further out to Ryland's Nook that wasn't too far from the River Trent's path through the Derbyshire countryside. At other times, he would be out nesting for eggs, "In those days there was nothing wrong with egg collecting, most lads had an egg collection, and we would compare whose was the best, who had the biggest, or the smallest, the best collection or the rarest egg. There wasn't much that scared me and I was the biggest of all of us, which came in handy when I scaled right to the top of the trees. I always managed to bag a good egg." Sport was an unrivalled passion of Nigel's but after it came fishing and there were plenty of ponds around Coton, as well as the Trent tributaries where he could get a couple of hours fishing in after school with some of his mates. If there was no football or cricket at the weekend, he could take off from dawn till dusk and think nothing of a six-mile walk to the Trent. Nigel's skill as a fisherman brought good fortune to the family and he would regularly bring home a freshly-caught trout for the dinner table, a treat that was welcomed as Great Britain was at war with Germany. Rationing was harsh and there was no guarantee there would be supplies in the village shop. Trout were fairly easy to come by, but Nigel had always wanted to land a pike, as he'd been with his cousin a few times when he had managed to pull one out. "This one day I got a bite but he was giving me a bit of a run-around. Uncle Charlie had to help me get this three-foot monster onto the bank, I got it unhooked but then it turned and came thrashing towards me and nearly managed to get a hold of my fingers with its teeth like knives. Charlie whipped out his knife and shoved it into its head. I had landed a pike; I didn't need to do it again." Sometime later, but before another fishing trip, Mother told my Father 'not to come back home until Nigel has been taught how to swim.' She was always concerned when I went out in case I had an accident. Like most lads I was drawn to the lakes and waters about. Well, on this one day we set off to a favourite spot. There was Uncle Charlie and me, my Dad, my cousin and my brother George. Us lads carried the fishing gear as usual and we set off on the three-mile trek to get there. As soon as we arrived, I set to making the hooks with the pins Mother had given us. Dad seemed extra-interested how long it was taking and kept asking, 'Are you done lad?' As soon as the last one was put on the line Dad shouted up, 'now's the time!' George and Charlie were on me like a shot and grabbed hold of an arm and a leg each and before I realised what was happening they swung me up high over the bank and threw me straight into the river. I flapped for all I was worth, frantically trying to keep my head from going under, mouthfuls of filthy tasting water had me retching and all the time I thought, 'this is it, I'm going to drown' but somehow I managed to kick and scramble my way back to the edge. I crawled through the mud and lying down fighting to catch my breath I heard Dad pipe up 'thee can swim better than me lad!' I guess that was the day he made sure I could swim."

Nigel wasn't short of mates and a few privileged friends accompanied him to his Uncle's workplace. As an estate manager of a nearby country mansion, Nigel's Uncle had access to some quality private fishing lakes, "We felt like royalty up there and the fishing wasn't bad either"

Sundays were for worship and this was the one day when everything else took a back seat. "It was church in the morning and then I'd stay on for afternoon Sunday school. After the family Sunday dinner, I would go back to church with a few mates; we were in the choir and had a great time. Being a choirboy had its perks!" One perk was that the local squire of nearby Catton Hall would throw open the gates to his estate annually for all the parishioners and hold a huge picnic with events and games. It was a day of fun and merriment for a village that was mostly quiet and sedate.

When the Second World War broke out, Nigel was still fairly young, but can still remember hearing the bombs dropping close to the house. Fradley was a village just about eight miles west of Coton-in-the-Elms and had a large airfield and aerodrome where English bombers were stationed. This became a target for the German Luftwaffe and they would fly over dropping bombs on Fradley, trying to destroy the stationary bomber planes and render the airfield useless. Just on the outskirts of Coton were some pretty impressive spotlights and anti-aircraft guns, which were harassing the enemy. The Germans were keen to take out these threats and so Coton village became a target for the bombing raids - but one that managed to survive.

As time passed Nigel outgrew the little Coton football outfit and in 1947 he moved on and started playing for a newly-formed team Stapenhill FC who were known locally as the 'Swans.' The 'Swans' played their matches at Stapenhill, a suburb of Burton-on-Trent in Staffordshire. He played every Saturday; one away game was against the Pirelli Factory team and years later he learned that the Pirelli ground was re-developed and became the new stadium for the Football League side Burton Albion. Nigel put in a great shift in goal that day; good enough to catch the eye of legendary Wolverhampton Wanderers scout Charlie Wheeler. When the game finished Charlie paid a visit to the Sims' household and asked Nigel and his parents if he would like to go to the Wanderers for a trial. Nigel could hardly contain himself, "Would I, you don't need to ask twice" and he jumped at the chance. Nigel went off to Wolves for the trial and when called into goal he found himself up against a local factory side, it didn't go well and the Wolves were hammered 7-0. The following week, in his second trial match, Wolves lost again 4-0; this time away to near rivals Walsall. Nigel could see his chance slipping away and wasn't surprised when he didn't hear from Wolves again. A dream come true had ended before it had hardly begun. However someone at Molineux must have seen something they liked in the young goalkeeper. As the 1947/48 season drew to a close, Nigel received a telegram inviting him back. Sims' latest game was a Birmingham League fixture against Stourbridge FC at Molineux. The 'Glassboys,' as they were known, were a local outfit but they knew their game and had previously won the Birmingham League Championships, as well as the Worcestershire and Herefordshire Senior Cups. They gave a good account of themselves against the Wanderers' big boys also making sure the goalkeeper had a good workout. When the final whistle blew, the Wolves Manager Stan Cullis approached young Sims and congratulated him on an impressive display. Stan asked Nigel if he would like to join the ground staff, "Well what do you say to that then. It was like winning the pools, and I said yes."

CHAPTER TWO

I'M A WANDERER

Leaving Coton-in-the-Elms was a bittersweet experience for both Nigel and his parents. He was sad to be saying goodbye to home and village life. It had been the only place he had ever known for the past seventeen years and this big step had him feeling extremely happy and excited, but at the same time he was slightly nervous at the idea of moving up to Wolverhampton with all that big city life might throw at him. He had only ever wanted one thing in life and that was to be a professional footballer. Now he had his foot on the first rung of what he hoped would turn out to be a very long ladder.

Jack and Edith Sims were hopeful and happy for their son because they knew how much it meant to him having this opportunity. It was all he had ever wanted, but they were well aware of the reality that only a small minority of lads would go on to make a career out of professional football. "From being ten or eleven-years-old I would eat, breathe and sleep football, it was my burning ambition and I wanted it more than anything else. It's all I thought about and then the day came, my father drove me up to Wolverhampton and that's where it all started."

Nigel was placed in his new digs along with the four other new intakes: Johnny Walker, Ken Whitfield, John Short and Ian Clark. "The place we stayed at was a bit like a hostel and it was run by a Mr and Mrs Lowharch." The accommodation was organised by the Wolves and the football club employed the couple. Their role was to offer a relaxed home environment for the latest crop of apprentices and ground staff that came to Molineux each year. "They really were a lovely couple and they took great care of all us youngsters, while the older and more established players were housed elsewhere." There was one lad in particular that Nigel got on well with at the digs and this was the young Scottish inside-forward Johnny Walker. Walker's Wolves career would almost mirror Nigel's time at Molineux; however Johnny found his first team appearances severely restricted. He would go on to start only forty-four first team games although he scored an astonishing twenty-six times. In his first dozen appearances Walker scored eight goals. It was remarkable performances like these that would underline exactly what strength in depth the Wolves had in their squad at the time. "I was surrounded by England internationals," Walker said. "I would love to have played more games for the Wanderers but I was forced out of the reckoning by some very talented players. Billy Wright, Jesse Pye, Johnny Hancocks, Jimmy Mullen and Dennis Wilshaw were all there when Stan Cullis first picked me in 1949/50. Peter Broadbent and Norman Deeley arrived later, and with Bill Slater and Ron Flowers breaking through over the next few years, what a collection of talent that was!"

Nigel Sims joined Wolverhampton Wanderers on £4 per week as a member of the 'ground staff'; his chores had to be done before football training could start at three o'clock in the afternoon, when all the other players had gone home. Mondays were his busiest day if the first team had played at home that weekend. His work would consist of sweeping away match day programmes littering the terracing. These programmes were basically just a few pages listing the starting XI, (today's price for this 1940s 'litter' can be anywhere between £25-£30!) He would also clean the first team players' boots, clear the dressing rooms and scrub the floors and toilets.

At that time Joe Gardiner, the former Wolves defender, was the head trainer and five assistants aided him. He would coach the youngsters three nights a week on top of their afternoon sessions. In the evening the fifteen-year-old ground staff lads would get the same training sessions as England captain Billy Wright. "You had to have something about you just to get noticed at the Wolves in them days; they were a top, top side and had finished in third position in the First Division the previous season," Nigel recalls. Each year trials would be arranged for about one-hundred and fifty handpicked youngsters who had been selected by the Wolverhampton club's scouting network. This network spread as far north as Scotland and right down to the West Country. Only a third of these trialists would go on to flourish under the club's guidance and a few lucky ones showing real potential would be offered professional terms. The club would have up to forty professionals on the books at any one time, ranging from seventeen to thirty-six-year-olds.

At the tender age of sixteen, Jimmy Mullen would play in the Cup Semi-Final and then go on to play in the first team for the next twenty years. "For a kid like myself, it was a big eye-opener; everything was very impressive and was geared for success. The one thing that stands out all these years later was the sign above the dressing room doors which read, 'There is no substitute for hard work'."

After six or seven months Nigel's eagerness, combined with his ability, would earn him a professional contract. The mundane tasks around the ground would cease and he would be able to concentrate on full-time training as a footballer. An additional bonus with signing 'pro forms' was a modest wage increase to £7 a week.

Pre-season training at Wolves and many other professional teams of the time would begin with the players reporting back to the club and having their weight recorded. This gave the coaching staff a good idea of "who had behaved themselves and kept their playing weight stable and who hadn't bothered!"

As well as regular football, cricket games were introduced very early on and these formed the basis of the first weeks of pre-season training. Matches would be played between the first team and the youngsters. Nigel had played plenty of cricket as a child in Coton and he was a very accomplished fast bowler. He liked to model his game on the great Yorkshire fast bowler 'Fiery' Freddie Trueman and Lancashire's Brian Statham. As a youngster with no television set in the house his ear would be permanently glued to the family wireless listening with admiration to BBC test match cricket commentator John Arlott and the broadcasting skills of Raymond Glendenning who covered the FA Cup Finals from 1946 to 1963.

His fast bowling ability in these training sessions would make an impression on the staff at the Wolves and he impressed early amongst the new arrivals. Nigel had maintained his strength and kept his fitness sharp by training repeatedly throughout the close season.

"I remember one training session where they were practising floating crosses over and as I came out to collect the ball I was bundled into the net; I'd been shoulder charged, which was perfectly legit in those days." Stan Cullis had seen this and gave the young 'keeper a dressing down: "You catch, and then get out of your goal! Catch and out! Catch and out!" That was the first and last time Nigel would get 'caught out' like that.

As a newcomer to the club, the highest level of football that Nigel could expect to play would be turning out for the third team, as "only on the odd occasion would a newcomer manage to get a game in the reserve side."

At this time Nigel was having problems with his feet and took the difficult decision to have surgery. He was seventeen at the time and life as a professional footballer was just starting to unfold, undergoing operations on both feet in order to resolve complications with his Achilles tendons was a hard choice. Luckily this was a minor hiccup in his career and the treatment was successful. After a short recovery period Nigel was eased back into full-time training.

For Nigel it was train, train, train, and sometimes there was a payoff. "I hadn't been at Wolves that long and I remember travelling up with the reserves for a game at Blackpool. We stayed at the Queens Hotel in Manchester and after lunch we were making our way to the ground on the coach. There was a mad scramble at the back of the bus and it turned out that Ted Elliot the goalkeeper had gone down with food poisoning. I had no choice, and I had to go in goal. The older lads playing in defence would talk me through that day, 'Your ball' they kept shouting. Bill Slater the centre-half played against me that day; he went on to become an England international and a few years later he became a teammate at the Wolves. This would be about 1953."

After this Nigel found himself playing regularly for the reserves. He kept giving good performances between the posts and was rewarded with his long awaited first team debut. On April 18th 1949, Easter Monday, Sheffield United were hosting the Wolves at Bramall Lane. United were sitting eighteenth in the Division, four places from the bottom while the Wolves were up in eighth position. Regular 'keeper Bert Williams had picked up an injury earlier in the month but he had still been expected to take his place in the starting eleven. When Manager Stan Cullis realised that Williams couldn't play he sent for his replacement goalkeepers to be driven up from the Midlands. Don Everall, who owned the coaches that transported the team, drove Nigel and another 'keeper, Dennis Parsons, up to Sheffield in his car. Nigel assumed that the older player Parsons would be starting, so he was still sitting in the dressing room thumbing through the match day programme when Cullis stalked in, "What the hell are you doing? Get your strip on!"

"I didn't even know I was playing." Nigel said. "I remember I couldn't hear the ref's whistle with all the noise the crowd was making and at the time not being able to hear was a big worry, but you know what, the more games you played, it just sort of became second nature and you could block out the noise, even when you played in front of a 50,000-strong crowd! The funniest thing was my Father was there before the game and he asked our full-back Roy Pritchard if he could look after me during the game." Roy told me years after, "I told your Dad, I said, look after him? He's much bloody bigger than me!"

The game finished 1-1 and Nigel was pleased with his contribution, playing behind such household names of the times as Billy Wright, Jesse Pye and Jimmy Dunne with Johnny Hancocks and Jimmy Mullen on the wing. He retained his place for the next day's home clash when Wolves trounced Sheffield United 6-0, keeping a clean sheet. The following Saturday he started his third game in only six days, Wolves were held to a 1-1 draw with fifth-placed Manchester City at Molineux. A home win would have been sufficient for Wolves to leapfrog City but the draw meant they remained in seventh place.

Nigel was not included in the side for the following weeks FA Cup Final showdown at Wembley against Leicester City - something he had known about the previous weekend. The victorious Wanderers beat their East Midlands rivals 3-1, with Jesse Pye scoring two goals and Sammy Smyth adding the other.

"I was more physically imposing and dominant than Bert Williams. Bert said we had, 'completely different styles'." During his Molineux years Nigel noticed that he would be called into the side if their opponents had a big burly type of centre-forward who had the reputation of shoulder charging goalkeepers into the net, "It seemed that I would get the Nat Lofthouses and Trevor Fords of the world." Surprisingly Nigel wasn't there to see his teammates win the Cup at Wembley; the club hadn't invited him to travel to London.

That season he made one more appearance, in the final game of the season against Chelsea. It was a 1-1 draw. Wolves finished the 1948/49 season in sixth position in Division One.

Later in the year Nigel was called up for National Service. Just before getting his call-up papers the National Service duration was increased from eighteen months to two years. "I was sickened. Two years nowadays feels like ten minutes, back then it felt like a lifetime." Initially he was based at Rhyl where he completed the six-week basic training, then moved to serve the remainder of his time at the Shropshire town of Oswestry, which was a lot closer to Wolverhampton. Someone at Wolves had connections in high places. Of course this meant he was still able to train with his teammates but even though he was available to play matches he would only turn out once for the first team in the next two years.

While serving at Oswestry, Nigel still managed to keep his competitive hand in and turned out for Western Command. Other notable players in the Army at that time were 'Big John' Charles who turned out for the Northern Area and Tommy Taylor who represented the Eastern Area, Nigel played against both of these famous footballers.

While based in Shropshire, Nigel managed an appearance in the Wolves third team against Oswestry. During the game a shot came in and as Nigel dived to smother the ball, his teammate the Wolves full-back Len Gibbons had also 'gone in' putting his foot in attempting to 'cut the ball out.' As Nigel came down he landed accidentally on the defenders leg and "felt it go."
"I was right upset about it, Len was a good lad and I knew straight away he was in obvious pain and in a bad way. Cullis came over and he was furious. He was shouting and waving his arms. 'You're finished, you are,' he said, shouting all over the place that he would see to it I didn't go to South Africa with the team. Cullis was referring to the Wolves post-season tour; the Army had only just got in touch with Wolves to let them know I could go."

Whilst on National Service, Nigel played for the Army football team, who spent a lot of time in London. They even played matches 'against the enemy' in Germany, in the Olympic stadium in Berlin. "It was falling down, but it was a magnificent stadium in its old days, and we went to see 'The Wall.' The Army would send a team over every summer and the Germans were lovely to us, they looked after us superbly and couldn't have been better hosts."

In 1950 and with National Service coming to an end, Nigel turned out for an Army XI against the Irish FA XI; the game was played at Aldershot. Then finally his Army days were done, and he could concentrate fully on working his way back into the Wolves first team.

The 1951/52 season didn't start with great promise for Nigel; Wolves had already played eleven matches before he got the nod to play at Stoke City, where Stanley Matthews inspired the home side to a 1-0 victory. His next appearance was relatively soon, only three weeks later. Again Wolves went down, more comprehensively this time, with a 4-1 defeat at home to Tom Finney's Preston North End who prior to kick off, had been sitting comfortably in sixth position. "Before the game Stan Cullis went to great lengths briefing the defence. We had to make sure at all costs that Finney who was the Preston outside-right and seen as the biggest threat, was stopped from playing his normal game which was going down the wing and putting in dangerous crosses. Orders were to 'make him cut inside onto his weaker left side as he is rubbish on his left,' so what happens? The first time he comes up against our left-half, Tom's way is blocked. Cut off from tearing down the wing he shimmies left, makes a bit of space inside for himself and wallop! Right into the top corner of the bloody net!"

Nigel would appear only twice more that season. Wolves had struggled and were glad to see the season end, finishing in a lowly sixteenth place.

Nigel remarked to his boss Cullis that he didn't care too much for playing in the reserves at this stage of his career, "You're too good for the reserves? Well we can soon sort that out!" Cullis promptly dropped Sims to the third string, where he would have remained had 'keeper Williams avoided injury.

The 1952/3 season would be the kind the aspiring village 'keeper had dreamed of during those long winter days, sitting on bare floorboards in his bedroom, bouncing and catching, bouncing and catching until he could see tennis balls with his eyes shut. Wolves would end the season in third position but what really pleased Nigel was that he would make more starts for the Wanderers that season than in all the previous five years he had spent at Molineux.

He wasn't called upon until the thirteenth game of the season (it certainly wasn't unlucky thirteen for Nigel), and only managed four appearances before the New Year. In November Nigel played against Manchester City when Wolves beat them 7-3 at home. Nigel was close friends with City's German-born goalkeeper Bert Trautmann and after the match they met up in the player's lounge. Bert came up to Nigel and they put their arms round each other. All the other players chorused, "They've been together now for forty years!" Nigel remembered, "It was funny, it always makes me smile - Bert was a lovely person and a bloody good goalkeeper too!"

Nineteen-fifty-three continued and this was turning out to be Nigel's year. He came in to play an absolute blinder in a 3-0 win at Old Trafford in February; this win taking Wolves up to second place in the table, breathing down Burnley's neck who were only one point ahead. Retaining his place, Nigel turned out the following week when Wolves were held to a 1-1 draw at home to Newcastle United; but one point wasn't enough to hold on to second position. Nigel managed two games on the bounce and then added another seven matches. It wasn't until April 11th when he was finally displaced. In those nine games he kept four clean sheets and Wolves would lose only once and take maximum points in five of them. Nigel signed off his 1952/53 season on April 6th with a 2-2 draw against Portsmouth at Molineux. Wolves that day sat proudly at the top of Division One! Without Nigel in their last three games the Wolves would win only once, concede five goals but worse still would drop two places down the table to finish third overall. It poses the question, "If only?"

The following year would see a vast improvement, and by the end of the season Wolves would be crowned Champions for the first time in their seventy-seven-year history. However it was scant reward for Nigel who would only play in nine matches. Had Stan Cullis allowed him to appear once more that season Nigel would have qualified for a Championship medal.

"Maybe the decision to make 'The Great Escape' and abscond from our enforced recuperation in Ireland was what made Stan dislike me so much and stopped me getting the Championship medal. It was sometime in the summer in 1953, anyway I was sent over, along with Bobby Mason and Ron Stockin to Ireland, I had tonsillitis and Mason was sent because the management thought he needed a bit more meat on his bones. I never knew why Stockin was sent over there with us but anyway, we stayed in this little hotel in Bray and we were there for a week or so. Well, I just couldn't stand it anymore, they were feeding us on salad and potatoes for every meal and Mason was never going to put weight on as long as we stayed there. There was nothing going on and nothing to do, so we decided to go back home. We caught the ferry back and thought no more of it. Then we were summoned to Molineux by letter and had to go up in front of Stan Cullis and three Directors. As much as Cullis wanted to throw the book at us, me especially, the Directors were more lenient as we hadn't really done anything wrong."

The new season, 1953/54, could have started better for the Coton-born 'keeper. He had started in all five opening fixtures, but Wolves had taken maximum points in only three of them, having had a very difficult start with their first three games away, a 4-1 defeat at Turf Moor on the opening day, Maine Road three days later, where they won convincingly 4-0 and then a long trip up to the north-east to Sunderland's Roker Park, to return empty handed in a 3-2 reversal.

By September Nigel found his familiar place on the bench and sat that and the next three months out, right through to Christmas Eve, a run of eighteen games. He would come back into the side to face Aston Villa twice: The first being in a 2-1 home defeat with the return fixture being played just forty-eight hours later at Villa Park where the result would be reversed, Wolves going home with both points. The two games together pulled in a total crowd just short of 90,000. After the win at Villa Park Cullis told Nigel, "I'm very pleased that's come!" He was obviously happy to have put one over on their fierce rivals; praise indeed was to follow when he told Nigel, "You are making enormous strides." That was to be the only time Stan Cullis managed positive words to his 'keeper.

Nigel remained in the side for the next two games, the first a 3-1 win over the 'Bluebirds' at Ninian Park, Cardiff followed by his only ever FA Cup appearance for Wolverhampton Wanderers. Unfortunately they were defeated 2-1 at home by bitter Midlands rivals Birmingham City.

That season Wolverhampton Wanderers would show the football world just how important it was to have strength in depth. While the first team were toasting their first-ever Division One Championship (they had been runners-up on three previous occasions), the reserves lifted the Central League title, the third team would 'take' the Birmingham League and the fourth team would capture the Worcestershire Combination to secure a clean sweep.

During the next two seasons at the Wolves, Nigel made only eight more appearances. These would turn out to be his last, giving him a not so grand total of thirty-nine games played.

In 1954, Nigel Sims would play only a paltry five matches for the Wolves yet he was still chosen to play in the traditional Eve of Cup Final fixture at Highbury on Friday April 30th. Here Nigel represented Young England v England. The 'old timers' won 2-1, with goals from Mannion and Lawton. Hines netted the 'youngsters' goal. The teams that day were: -

England	Young England
1 Bartram (Charlton)	1 Sims (Wolves)
2 Mozley (Derby county)	2 Sillett (Chelsea)
3 Smith L. (Arsenal)	3 Byrne (Manchester Utd)
4 Johnston (Blackpool)	4 Adamson (Burnley)
5 Leuty (Notts County)	5 Smith T. (Birmingham C)
6 Cockburn (Manchester Utd)	6 Edwards (Manchester Utd)
7 Matthews (Blackpool)	7 Hooper (West Ham Utd)
8 Mannion (Middlesbrough)	8 Quixall (Sheffield Wed)
9 Lawton (Arsenal)	9 Hines (Leicester City)
10 Shackleton (Sunderland)	10 Viollett (Manchester Utd)
11 Langton (Blackburn Rovers)	11 Pilkington (Burnley)

It was a special day for Sims because he would play against his boyhood hero Leon Leuty who had been a defender for Nigel's favourite team Derby County.

In 1955, during his last full year with the Wanderers, he went on the club's pre-season tour to Moscow and played in several of their glamorous floodlit friendlies. Wolves had been one of the first sides in the country to have floodlights installed, in 1953, and it was partly down to their involvement in these prestigious 'floodlit' fixtures against famous world clubs such as Real Madrid, Valencia, Borussia Dortmund, Spartak Moscow, Racing Club of Argentina and the live BBC televised game versus Honved of Hungary that would ultimately lead towards the founding of the UEFA Champions League, formerly the European

Cup. That season Nigel would turn out on just five more occasions for the first team.

Deep down Nigel knew things at Molineux would never be any different. Again he would be driven down to a game, a 2-2 draw at Highbury played during the Christmas period, in Don Everall's car. It was another last-minute appearance due to Williams not being able to play, much the same as Nigel's debut circumstances at Bramall Lane six years earlier. Four days later, on New Year's Eve Nigel retained his place in the 0-2 reversal at home to Cardiff City. Playing yet again in quick succession, Nigel travelled up to the north-east to Roker Park to play his last-ever away game for the Wolves. Twelve weeks before, Sunderland had smashed the transfer record to bring Welsh international centre-forward Trevor Ford up from the Midlands. This player's move from Aston Villa had cost the 'Mackems' the princely sum of £30,000. During the match a low ball came zipping in from the wing. As Nigel dived down to gather it, Ford whacked out with his foot, and completely missing the ball, he ripped the entire length of Nigel's shorts.

Nigel would have to wait a month and a half since the 1-1 draw at Sunderland to make his next, what would turn out to be his final appearance, for the 'Old Golds' of Wolverhampton. Unfortunately the curtain would come down on his Molineux career with a fiercely-fought 2-0 defeat at the hands of Matt Busby's Manchester United. Nigel Sims signed off with Wolverhampton Wanderers sitting in third position in Division One.

Bert Williams had regularly threatened to retire, but nothing ever came of it and Nigel was beginning to realise that his future was in his own hands and possibly elsewhere…

CHAPTER THREE

RISE AND SHINE

In March 1956 Nigel was summoned to Molineux. Two gentlemen had arrived and wanted to see him, so he was taken from the stadium to a small café nearby. The visitors were Aston Villa Manager Eric Houghton and the Club Secretary Fred Archer and they were looking to speak privately with Nigel. Eric asked, "We want you to come to the Villa - how do you feel about that?" Nigel was taken with the idea and mulled it over.

Things had changed in Midlands' football over the last few years. When World War Two broke out the Football League's Division One was suspended and did not resume until peacetime in 1946. By 1955 Wolverhampton Wanderers were a force to be reckoned with and a stronger outfit than their other local rivals. They finished higher than Aston Villa in eight of those nine seasons. In that time the Wanderers were crowned Champions once and runners-up twice. Although this was an impressive record, Nigel could see he wasn't going to fulfil his potential at the club and it was time to move on. Career-wise, it could have been said that Nigel was taking a step down, but this wasn't the case at all and he knew only too well that a team was only as good as its last game. Aston Villa may not have featured at the top of the Division during that time, but it hadn't been all Wolves. In their last season Villa had been involved in seven FA Cup ties. Teams can land the trophy playing as little as six matches. Villa only reached the fourth round where Doncaster Rovers knocked them out; the initial game being drawn at Doncaster and the replay at Villa Park also being level at full-time. It took three further replays to reach its conclusion.

With his thinking done he had a smile and an answer, "I'd love to. Where do I sign?" Unknown to Nigel, Stan Cullis had given the nod to the Villa giving them permission to talk to the 'keeper. So it looked like the deal was done and Nigel's 'Wandering' days were over! Nigel was invited to watch the following Saturday's game at Villa Park - the FA Cup Semi-Final

41

between Manchester City and Tottenham Hotspur.

For Aston Villa times were changing and in the previous 54/55 season Danny Blanchflower and Tommy Thompson requested and were granted transfers. Villa also lost two of their longest-serving players, Harry Parkes and Frank Moss. Both had played in excess of three-hundred first team games. Parkes would leave to develop his sports outfitting business based in Corporation Street, Birmingham, while Frank Jr would leave to pursue his hobby of breeding pigs.

With all of these comings and goings, Villa needed to turn the tide of their fortune, so they set about spending big money and bringing in major new signings. Les Smith, Jimmy Dugdale and finally Nigel joined early season arrivals, Pat Saward and Jackie Sewell in the New Year.

The new additions fitted seamlessly into a side that would only get better as the campaign progressed. Luckily the majority of the club's established players - Stan Lynn, Peter Aldis, Peter McParland and captain Johnny Dixon - would remain relatively injury-free. This would turn out to be crucial later in the season due to the Villa's lacklustre start.

With only one win in their first fourteen matches of the new 55/56 campaign Aston Villa were sitting in a dismal nineteenth place with only nine points gained, two points below Arsenal and Manchester City. With a one point advantage Sheffield United were sitting one place above the Villa, Cardiff City were on equal points. Huddersfield Town were one point and two places below and propping everyone else up were Tottenham Hotspur with only five points to show for their efforts. Only Huddersfield Town and Arsenal had scored fewer than the fifteen goals that Villa had managed. The poor League placing was down to the fact that the 'Villans' had conceded nearly two goals per game, managing to keep only three clean sheets.

Aston Villa would play nineteen more matches before the

arrival of Nigel. Of these, Villa won only five, they averaged a fraction over a goal a game, failed to score in seven, while in defence, conceded thirty-six goals, again close to two goals per game and managed only another three clean sheets.

At the beginning of December they returned from Bramall Lane with only a solitary point against fellow strugglers the 'Blades' in a 2-2 draw, after conceding an interval lead. Huddersfield proved a far better game for the Villa. The 'Terriers' returned to West Yorkshire with 'nowt' to show for their efforts other than a 3-0 drubbing at Villa Park. Stan Lynn scored, but the Villa's saviour after netting a brace was skipper Johnny Dixon.

As the New Year approached it was apparent that these three sides would be fighting it out with each other for their First Division survival. 'Spurs' were on the same nineteen points as the Villa and there was a good chance they might join the scrap. Sheffield United had a point less, while Huddersfield were slightly more adrift with sixteen. Cardiff City were in eighteenth place and had a three-point cushion on the teams below so it looked like they might be safe from relegation.

Late on the Friday evening of March 16th 1956, Nigel Sims narrowly missed the transfer deadline when he signed for his new employers - Aston Villa Football Club. Signing for the Villa on the same night was the Walsall 'keeper Vincent McBride, who had been restricted to eleven first team starts for the 'Saddlers' in the two years he had been there. Nigel finally left Molineux (where he played second fiddle for eight years) in the shadow of Bert Williams. Now he was the new boy, though not so much of a boy at the age of twenty-four, but the new boy all the same. Already standing in his way between the Villa goal posts was the Welsh international stopper Keith Jones and next to him, Michael Pinner, the second choice. Pinner had deputised as recently as the previous month while Jones was injured, in a 1-0 defeat away, against Bolton Wanderers. When Nigel arrived at the club Jones was only two games shy of reaching two-hundred first team appearances for the Villa.

Nigel waited less than a week before making his debut and pulling on the famous 'Claret and Blue' jersey, or in his case, a green one! His Aston Villa career that would run for nearly the next decade would begin on Monday March 19th 1956 at home to Burnley, just two days after Villa Park played host to the FA Cup Semi-Final between the eventual winners Manchester City and Tottenham Hotspur. As a guest of the club for that semi-final, Nigel was able to get a glimpse of what the future might hold, "Villa Park was a fantastic stadium and on that day it was packed with 70,000 people and what an atmosphere! I couldn't wait to get out there and play in front of that massive terrace behind the goal, the one the Villa fans called the 'Holte End.' Before this I had only played at Villa Park for the opposition and that was 'Wolves' who were deadly rivals, so you can imagine what that had been like. I knew from experience how intimidating it could be for the visiting team, so God only knew what it was like when they were on your side!"

As Villa started the game against Burnley's 'Clarets' at the bottom of the table, things looked bleak. Only 15,120 fans bothered to turn out to watch the game, a far lower than anticipated gate. The match being put back forty-eight hours, due to Villa hosting its thirteenth FA Cup Semi-Final tie the previous Saturday, may have affected the size of the crowd. This low gate would turn out to be by far the Villa's lowest crowd that season, their average attendance a much healthier 29,968. Villa went in at the interval two goals to the good, thanks to strikes from Dixon and Smith, and as there were no more goals in the second-half, Villa took the points. Unfortunately it made no difference to their position as Huddersfield Town also won their weekend game at Leeds Road, with Everton the victims.

Nigel would go on to play in the following eight remaining fixtures that season. At Luton, Villa lost 2-1, although Geordie Tommy Southren netted one of only eight goals he scored in his time at the club. This defeat was quickly followed by a 2-0 win at home to Everton, the gate that day nearly double the Burnley match just 12 days earlier. This win would lift the Villa up a single place and off the basement of Division One to twenty-first place, but it still wasn't a position of safety and the Villa would need to dig deeper. Over the Easter period the Villa played two 'derby' games in as many days, the fixtures against 'Wolves' attracting a combined attendance in excess of 72,500. Nigel added two more clean sheets to his season's tally in those 'local grudge matches' but the Villa didn't push that little bit more to take advantage and score. These 0-0 draws were then followed by the Villa losing by the odd 'one' in a seven-goal classic at White Hart Lane. This kept the 'Villans' deep in the relegation area with just three games left in which to reach safety.

Knowing that a win was vital, and with the end of the season in sight, Sheffield United came down to Birmingham. They were only three points better off than the Villa but had the added luxury of two games in hand. Derek Pace scored his only ever hat-trick in a Villa shirt, and what a time to do it! It put a huge dent in the 'Blades' hopes of staying up. Final score: - Pace 3, Sheff Utd 2. 'Doc' Pace was also the hero at Preston North End's Deepdale ground, scoring the only goal in Villa's 1-0 win. The final match of the campaign brought the 'Baggies' to Villa. Willed on by their third-biggest home gate of the season, a whopping 42,876, they blasted three goals past the Albion with no reply in this demolition. Leslie Smith would hit a double, while Albion's unfortunate left-back Len Millard would put into his own net. Those maximum points in the last three games were vital, as survival went right down to the wire. The points meant the Villa would overhaul Huddersfield Town on goal average only.

Both sides finished on thirty-five points, but Villa's goal average was 0.75 against the 'Terriers' 0.65, this was the closest finish since the 50/51 season when Chelsea stayed up at the expense of Sheffield Wednesday by virtue of 0.04 of a goal! Villa finished in the not so lofty position of twentieth but at least safety was achieved and top-flight football was guaranteed for next season. It had been an instantly forgettable campaign. Aston Villa had scored the fewest goals in the Division and captain Johnny Dixon was the only player to reach 'double figures.'

The Villa Chairman Chris Buckley, a former club centre-half, came out publicly stating the obvious, that there was "work to be done." He would also predict the Villa would be making headlines in the following season and not through relegation.

Nigel had rounded his season off with another clean sheet. This was a remarkable six 'shutouts' achieved in a run of only nine consecutive games. Somebody had obviously been paying attention to the art of goalkeeping in an era when football was played with five defenders and five forwards, the emphasis was on attack and high scoring affairs were the order of the day. For the first time in Nigel's career he found himself as the club's number one stopper. Keith Jones would go on to make only one more appearance for the first team with his career total being one-hundred and ninety-nine games.

Nigel had come late to the campaign; he was given a place in the starting eleven and held onto that position until the close of the season. In his book that was a job well done, "I was playing under Eric Houghton. He was a great manager who had the belief in me and he could see and appreciate the effort I would put into every game. He was a lovely chap and because he was always telling me that I was a great player I started to believe more in my ability, and it made me an even better goalkeeper. I think it was really strange how two managers (Eric Houghton and Stan Cullis) could be so different from each other. One couldn't stop giving praise and the other, well, he just wouldn't."

It had been a long time coming, but finally he had something to work towards. Where would this go? Was Nigel's star finally ready to rise and shine? Only time would tell.

CHAPTER FOUR

ONWARD AND UPWARD

In March 1956 The Grand Hotel in Birmingham was the venue for the Villa's eighty-first Shareholders AGM. There was unrest following a long season of flirtation with relegation and their playing style, or some would say a lack of it; being labelled, "a disgrace to the fine name of the club." An unsuccessful bid was made to remove directors Norman Smith and W E Lovsey.

Very few personnel changes occurred before the start of the new season, the notable exception being the departure of Con Martin, the centre-half who had also appeared in goal for the Villa on numerous occasions. Con decided to leave Villa Park and go back to his native Ireland to take an appointment with Waterford as a player/manager.

The new season kicked-off on Saturday August 18th with the Villa entertaining Charlton Athletic. Bill Baxter popped up that day to score one of only six goals in his time at the Villa, setting up a comfortable 3-1 win, a definite morale booster for the forthcoming campaign. Three games followed in August, two of them being against local rivals West Bromwich Albion, but Villa only managed to collect two points in the three fixtures.

At the start of September, Blackpool made their way down from the north-west, and the Villa's unbeaten home record remained intact for the time being. Peter McParland the Villa's Irish outside-forward scored a brace in the 3-2 win raising hopes that he would rediscover his shooting boots after netting a meagre four League goals in the previous campaign. September saw another four points collected from a further five matches. The best result of the season so far, the 4-0 victory up at Goodison Park. Everton had no answer that day and the Villa tore them apart, all goals coming in the second-half. Jackie Sewell showed the fans why he had been England's most expensive player just six years earlier; he weighed in with a double that afternoon to add to the one he had scored in their last home game. By the time the final whistle was blown Aston

Villa were sitting in a lofty fifth position. It was a good solid start; having an injury-free team and the same starting eleven certainly did them no harm. If that current form continued the Villa fans might well have something to cheer at the end of the season.

October started with a bit of a wobble and Villa lost heavily 5-1 on the south coast to Pompey. They found no way to contain Scottish international Jackie Henderson and his fellow forward Johnny Gordon, who each scored twice. Leslie Smith weighed in with Villa's solitary strike. The remaining games that month were a turnabout and brought some joy to the fans, and more importantly maximum points. Leslie Smith continued his scoring streak and smashed two past Newcastle United in a 3-1 win, Jackie Sewell bagged the other. The 'Magpies' conceded all three goals in the first forty-five minutes. Birmingham City's visit attracted an impressive 54,927 gate and the 'Claret and Blue' contingent went home the happier having witnessed their side put three into their bitter rivals' net, the 'Blues' only responding once. Sewell had scored for the second game on the trot along with Stan 'the wham' Lynn and Ken O Roberts, who scored his only goal of the season.

For Nigel, life was good, he had finally become the number one choice stopper at his club and he was content with his lot. He had played in every game and as long as he could steer clear of injury it looked like his run would just roll on and on. Nigel had finally realised a long-held boyhood ambition. "After all those wasted years at Molineux it felt good, it felt really good!"

November saw the Villa reap only four points out of a possible eight, with a solitary win at home to Burnley being the only highlight.

By December 8th Aston Villa were close to being midway through the season and were sitting comfortably mid-table, their opponents that day at Villa Park, Manchester United, were in pole position. United had finished eleven points clear of

Blackpool in the previous season to clinch the title and it was looking odds on that they would successfully defend their crown. There was already daylight at the top of the table with second-place Tottenham trailing them by four points and Leeds United a further two points behind. The goal that day came from 'Big Pat' Saward who knocked in the Villa's consolation, but it wasn't enough in a 3-1 reversal. 'Big Pat' had scored in the same fixture in the season before; in his entire Midland career he amassed one-hundred and seventy appearances, but only managed two goals. Vic Crowe played that day, a Welsh-born, Handsworth-raised redhead, and affectionately known to his teammates as 'Spike,' this was his only game of the entire 56/57 campaign. Vic would become a close friend of Nigel's over the years, "The Villa faithful (there were 42,530 spectators that afternoon) gave Vic such a loud, standing ovation when he made his way out of the tunnel and onto the pitch, you were left in no doubt how much the fans had taken to him, he was a battler and never gave up and the fans appreciated that."

Crowe a wing-half, was signed professionally by the Villa in 1952, and drafted into the first team in the October 1954 as stand-in for the injured Danny Blanchflower. Vic might have been waiting in the wings for some time, but when called up he hit the ground running. On Blanchflower's departure two months later, Crowe cemented the position as his own. He was a one-hundred per cent totally-committed tackler who shirked nothing; he'd already played sixty-four games in his first two seasons, and in later years was labelled an 'Aston Villa legend' who went on to write his name in the club's illustrious history. The following week Villa travelled to the capital to record their second away win of the season at the imposing home of Charlton Athletic, The Valley. Charlton were rooted firmly at the foot of the table and this was reflected in the disappointing crowd of only 13,452, who looked lost on the vast terracing which had held in excess of

75,000 in better times. 'Packy' McParland and skipper Johnny Dixon did the honours. Nigel kept a clean sheet to boot.

Villa's League record at this time showed a complete contrast between home and away form. At Villa Park they had won five, drawn three, lost two, scored seventeen and conceded thirteen. On their travels the Villa had won two, drawn three, lost five, scored thirteen and conceded sixteen.

Villa's next home game was Manchester City the following weekend, but was called off due to the weather. The next time they played was on Christmas Day when they met Sunderland at Roker Park. This 1-0 defeat was the last ever Christmas Day fixture for the Villa. Both teams travelled together by train for the reverse fixture at Villa Park the following day, but due to over half a foot of snow on the pitch the game was called off. The last game of the calendar year saw Villa travel to Blackpool where they came away with a satisfactory 0-0 draw. Blackpool had won eight of their home games prior to kick off and were sitting ten places higher in the League than their opponents.

Nigel made his twenty-second consecutive appearance in that match, something he didn't get anywhere close to at Wolves. He had kept his seventh clean sheet and he was thoroughly enjoying his football. He had a good solid dependable defence in front of him; because they were playing regularly as an unchanged outfit they were starting to play to their individual strengths and iron out any weaknesses. The defence were leaking fewer goals than last season but up front they were struggling to score again.

In defence Stan Lynn was the Villa's recognised right-back and had played eighty-four games over the last two seasons, but he'd been sidelined since March the previous season and had only returned to the team in September for the Bolton Wanderers' visit. Surprisingly he played up front in the number nine shirt. When he was reinstated to his familiar full-back berth, it looked like Lynn had never been away. The only downside was teammate and Stan's reliable cover for that period, Ray Hogg, would never see first team action again and would soon be on his way to Mansfield Town.

In the opposite berth, at left-back, was the evergreen dependable Peter Aldis; he had missed only one game since mid-October 1954, playing close to one-hundred matches in this time. He was not a prolific goal-getter; instead of being deemed 'a great scorer of goals'; the phrase 'a scorer of great goals' could have been coined especially for Peter. His solitary count in a career spanning two-hundred and ninety-five appearances was an amazing header fully thirty-five-yards from goal, with the luckless Sunderland on the receiving end.

Playing centre-half, the position recently vacated by former Holte End hero Con Martin, was Jimmy Dugdale. He had been drafted in for the tidy sum of £25,000 just ten months earlier from West Brom. 'The Laughing Cavalier' as he was affectionately known, had previously won an FA Cup winners medal in '54 whilst at the 'Baggies', but he had been displaced and found it difficult to get back in the team. Seeking pastures new, he made the short journey to Villa Park - Albion's loss was certainly Aston Villa's gain. Partnering Dugdale on the half-back line and playing as a right-sided wing-half was Villa's newest acquisition, nineteen-year-old local Bilston-born lad Stan Crowther. Stan had been snapped up, or stolen might be a better description, by Eric Houghton from Stan's home team, Bilston Town, for the bargain price of £750 in August just as the new season kicked-off. His career at the Villa would be far shorter than the majority of this newly-assembled Villa side, but he was an honest, hard-grafting underrated player, who would go on to earn England Under-23 caps and also League representative honours.

To complete Nigel's lines of defence was the big tough Irish left-half Pat Saward. Pat had only come in fifteen months earlier from Millwall where he had plied his trade in the lower Leagues. Initially Pat played inside-forward for the Villa, one of a couple of his favourite positions. This season he was fancied as a wing-half and replacement for Villa's Welsh international Vic Crowe who was injured and would miss almost the entire 56/57 campaign. Years later, during his time as a coach at Coventry City, Pat was credited with unearthing the unpolished gem and future European Cup and League Championship-winning captain Dennis Mortimer.

Alan Deakin, an ex-Villa teammate of Saward's, was in no doubt that Pat worked really hard at keeping his fitness levels up to scratch, "I remember we would knock off at dinnertime from a Villa Park training session and he would go home and start all over again. He had a stomach like a washboard and was immaculately dressed - sharp suits, shirts pressed to perfection, tie, the full works; he took a lot of pride in how he dressed and how he looked."

Stan Crowther remembered Pat sharing a house with centre-forward Dave Hickson. "Dave wasn't with us that long, he come from Everton for £17,500 in the September ('55), and then he was gone. It was a joke that the ink had hardly dried on the contract before he left. Anyway, while he was here, he shared a place with Pat and they were like chalk and cheese. One day Dave couldn't find his shoes; he wasn't that tidy and his stuff was all over the place in his room. He needed to get to training on time so he took the only pair of shoes he could lay his hands on. Unfortunately they were Pat's. He would have got away with it but Pat had to be at training as well, so here he comes a bit later, 'Pat the snappy well-groomed dresser' turning up in a pair of slippers! He was not a happy chap; in fact he came in with a face like thunder. Dave found himself off to Huddersfield Town not long after that. It might have been coincidence. Who knows?"

Responsibility for scoring would fall to Villa's five-man

forward-line. Mostly Derek 'Doc' Pace would wear the iconic number nine shirt, traditionally the centre-forward's, in this season. He had been playing for Bloxwich Strollers when former Villa full-back George Cummings discovered him. He signed for the Villa in September 1949 and got his first team call-up in the March of '51. He had to bide his time, as there was strength in depth in his chosen position, but he was sure his luck would change when Trevor Ford moved on in October 1950. He hadn't banked on Miller Craddock or Dave Walsh coming in; Walsh being signed from the Albion two months after Ford left. Pace had a fight on his hands for the position with both players. Bagging a century of goals for West Brom, it was Walsh who was seen as the ideal replacement for Trevor Ford. 'Doc' had a good goal scoring record throughout his career at the Villa, but it would never bring him the monopoly on that prestigious shirt.

There always was a battle for the No 9 shirt; it had been worn by a string of Villa legends and household names; Archie Hunter, John Devey, Harry Hampton, Billy Walker and 'Pongo' Waring. Collectively these players scored a phenomenal eight-hundred and seventy-nine goals for the Villa. The latest skirmish was between 'Doc' and Billy Myerscough, but this was by no means the only competition, just the most significant. Five different players pulled the shirt on that season, and Pace made more starts in it than Myerscough. This was Billy's first season playing for the Villa; he had been part of a deal that had taken Dave Walsh to Walsall previously.

In the 56/57 season, Johnny Dixon was the longest-serving player and captain of the Villa, and the preferred inside-left. Before the Villa, Dixon had been playing his football up in County Durham for a little known Non-League outfit, Spennymoor United, who graced the North-Eastern League. He'd made the move south, after writing to the Birmingham side requesting a trial. Then he made his debut for the 'Claret and

Blues' way back in April '46. Skilful and versatile, he had no problem slotting in anywhere among the attack, and played in four of the five roles up front during his Aston Villa time. He had started the season in his favoured spot but as Pace was sidelined by the end of September, Dixon stepped in and played up front until Pace returned in mid-December.

Playing outside Dixon on the left-wing was Irishman Peter McParland. Eric Houghton's predecessor George Martin signed Peter. He was into his fourth season with the team and getting a reputation as someone who didn't just make goals but as a player who would 'cut in' and score his own. The number eleven shirt may as well have had his name on it. Over on the other side of the attack were the two new Villa boys, Jackie Sewell and Leslie Smith. Jackie Sewell arrived at the Villa just a few weeks before the outside-right Smith.

Leslie Smith had been a former Wolves player, but decided to move to the Villa in February 1956. He had been restricted to making fewer than one-hundred appearances at Molineux, due to the fine form of Johnny Hancocks and Jimmy Mullen. He also played in the Wanderers' Championship-winning season, but like Nigel he didn't make enough appearances to claim a medal. Little did he know when signing for Villa that his former teammate Sims would be joining him at the same club just four weeks later. Smith was operating on the right flank and he cemented his place in that position in much the same fashion as left-winger McParland had.

Sewell came in midway through the previous season so he already had fifteen starts under his belt before the new campaign started. Like others in the attack, he made the position his own. He could always be counted on to bag a few goals for the team.

Jackie Sewell had some history with the Villa manager Eric Houghton. In 1951, Eric was the manager at Notts County. The Division One club Sheffield Wednesday made an offer of £34,500 for Jackie and signed him as the most expensive player in the history of English football. This smashed the previous record of £30,000 set the year before, when Sunderland, who were known as 'the Bank of England club' managed to prise Trevor Ford from the Villa. The north-east giants had earned this nickname by breaking the transfer record on no fewer than four occasions. Sewell and his new club, the 'Owls,' promptly went down to Division Two. He helped them get instant promotion but didn't hang around too long before being bought back by the manager who had let him go four years earlier. Eric Houghton had also moved on from Meadow Lane and 'come home' to Aston Villa where he had played from 1929 until 1947 as a favourite of the fans, amassing one-hundred and seventy goals in three-hundred and ninety-two appearances.

Kenilworth Road was the venue for Aston Villa's third round FA Cup tie. Luton Town had been promoted only the season before last after playing eighteen seasons in the second flight. The condition of the pitch was heavy underfoot, with mud, but this suited Villa's style of play more than their hosts and at half-time they were in the lead with Dixon obliging. This advantage was given away and by the final whistle it was 2-2 and back to the Midlands for a replay forty-eight hours later. Luton faced their latest nemesis before a crowd of just over 28,000, Johnny Dixon netted a brace and with no reply from the opposition the Hatters' involvement in 'The Cup' came to an end. Onward and upward!

The first League game of the New Year was a convincing 5-1 hammering of Everton at Villa Park. This totalled nine goals past the Merseysiders in the campaign. The win pushed the Villa up two places to thirteenth as before this game the Villa had won only one of their last seven games. During the game Nigel sustained an injury, which would rule him out of the following week's visit to White Hart Lane, and Keith Jones was drafted back into the side as his replacement.

The programme notes for this match mentioned Arthur Henry Sabin, a young and promising goalkeeper who had just signed professional forms on Wednesday January 2nd. He made his debut the following Saturday in Villa's FA Youth Cup fixture playing at Villa Park against Sheffield United, in a 4-4 draw.

Jones' last first team run out had been ten months previously in a 3-2 win up at St James' Park, Newcastle. Nigel was nursing an injury but he was looking forward to better things, "We had a good home League record and Villa were in the hat for the fourth round of the Cup, morale was okay. A defeat at the hands of 'Spurs' wasn't a great shock in all honesty, but conceding the three goals was. We'd only shipped two goals in our previous four matches. 'Spurs' had been sitting in second place just on the shoulder of Manchester United, before they met us, and if you look back in the records, we had conceded the fewest goals in the Division up till then, and that was including Busby's lot, so we were doing something right."

The following week Nigel was back in position between the posts. The Villa made a long trek up to the north-east to meet the least fashionable of the sides there, who also happened to play at the bleakest stadium - Middlesbrough at Ayresome Park, in the fourth round of the FA Cup. It wasn't one for the purists. 'Boro' had been relegated three seasons ago, but that was before they had discovered, for their forward-line, a local born lad; an unbelievable striker who would undoubtedly have walked into any side in Europe. His name was Brian Clough.

Stan Crowther remembered an incident that happened just before the game. "Eric Houghton was giving the lads his team talk in the dressing room; he pointed to our centre-half and said, 'Jimmy, this Clough lad, he's good with his left, he's good with his right, but apart from that he's bloody useless.' There was a loud bang from the rear of the dressing room, our 'keeper Nigel

Sims, who wasn't a small lad, had laughed so hard that he had fallen off the bench!" Houghton had been right about Clough being good, but good was an understatement on Eric's part. 'Cloughie' scored one-hundred and ninety-seven goals in two-hundred and thirteen appearances for Middlesborough, then moved up the coast to Wearside where his scoring feats at Sunderland were just as impressive - notching up fifty-four in just sixty-one matches. When warming up before kick-off, Nigel had some sound advice for the defenders, "Keep him quiet lads and we know we are in with a shout." Luckily for Villa, Clough and the majority of the 42,396 partisan crowd were kept quiet enough that afternoon. By half-time Clough and Bill Harris had scored one apiece, and the Villa were trailing with one from Leslie Smith; but Brian and his teammates couldn't silence the Villa in the second-half and the lads made the journey back to Birmingham safe in the knowledge that their 3-2 win, with additional second-half goals from Pace and Dixon, had secured them a place in Monday's midday live radio draw for the next round. The Villa outside-left, 'Packy' McParland would later class this performance as the Villa's best of the whole 56/7 Cup campaign.

Back in the League, the Villa went on to draw their next three games after the 'Spurs' defeat. This put them in a slightly lower position than they were comfortable with, but they had as many as three games in hand over some of the teams directly above them.

Immediately after their latest 0-0 away draw to Bolton Wanderers came the small matter of an FA Cup Fifth Round tie against Division Two strugglers Bristol City. It was a Villa Park match and it was taken that the lads had too much in their locker not to advance to the last eight at the expense of the 'Robins.' Cup fever had gripped Birmingham, and a whopping 63,099 crowd turned out to shout on their heroes, with a fair number travelling up from the West Country. City hadn't come to the Midlands just to make the numbers up, they had put four past fellow Division Two side Rotherham in the last round so what did they have to lose? They pushed the Villa all afternoon. Villa managed to break the deadlock through 'Doc' Pace, and City came back with an equaliser through their England international striker, John Atyeo. Then, seventeen minutes before time, Jackie Sewell put away a superb goal, which wrapped up the tie for Villa.

The sixth round draw made history that year when it was made live on television for the first time. The Villa had been waiting patiently to see who their opponents would be in the sixth round. There were six top-flight teams left in the 'hat' along with promotion contenders Nottingham Forest, who, led by former Villa legend Billy Walker, would be promoted in May, behind their local rivals Leicester City. The real sixth round shocker was the inclusion in the last eight of Bournemouth & Boscombe Athletic from Division Three South. They had managed to negotiate victories in the first three rounds against similar level opposition, but then they went to Molineux on a cold January afternoon and, against the odds, they beat 'Wolves' who were sitting in fourth position in the top-flight. People started to sit up and take notice. Surely this had just been a one off? By the fifth round these upstarts faced the mighty Tottenham Hotspur albeit at home. 'Spurs' were on the shoulder of leaders Manchester United, and they planned to give the south coast boys a thorough footballing lesson they would never forget. This was indeed fulfilled - in reverse - on a memorable day when Athletic played Jimmy Anderson's 'Spurs' off the park at Dean Court, coming away with a giant killing 3-1 victory. The town and all football neutrals went mad!

With the draw underway there was only one team the Villa wanted to avoid and that was Burnley. The last eleven visits to

Turf Moor in Lancashire had given at best a single draw. Finally there was just two balls left in the hat; Burnley were picked out first, and the Villa had the one fixture they desperately wanted to avoid. Peter McParland was quoted as saying that he had nearly choked on his dinner when he heard the draw. The following day when the players turned in for training, all talk was about the draw and the bogey that needed to be laid to rest. There was an optimistic atmosphere and everyone was as keen as mustard and couldn't wait for the first Saturday in March when the game was due to take place, "Well if we don't beat 'em now we'll have to do 'em in the final" remembered Stan Crowther.

For the time being, Cup football had to be put on the back burner whilst the Villa concentrated on 'bread and butter' League games, - there was a home game coming up against Portsmouth, who were languishing second off the bottom position, this match to be played before the Burnley tie. It was imperative that Villa picked up points from their games in hand, if not they could find themselves in a relegation battle yet again. However, fortune was on the Villa side that day and a Jackie Sewell brace, one in each half of the game, earned the Villa a point. Although the Villa gave away an interval lead, the point they managed to gain was enough to take them to twelfth position and above the Albion on goal average only, both sides had twenty-seven points on the board after twenty-eight games played.

At the same stage the season before, Villa were second off the bottom and had only collected nineteen points, they'd scored eight fewer goals and conceded sixteen goals more. Compare this and the extended Cup run and this season was looking up for the 'Villans.'

When the Burnley tie came round, the Villa took an impressive 10,000 of their 'Claret and Blue' army up to Turf Moor. Nigel remembered, "It was a bleak place at the best of times, I have never been there to play a game and seen the sun shining," but it would get worse. Injured Villa wing-half Bill Baxter had been ruled out since starting the Sheffield Wednesday game in December, but he made the trip up and tagged along with the Villa fans that were looking for the ground. The bowler hatted-defender, complete with his Villa jersey wrapped round his neck and giant rattle in his hand, arrived at the stadium but the doorman was having none of it and didn't believe that Bill was a player and not a fan. It took Bill's teammates going out to the gate to convince the chap that he was part of the squad. When Baxter finally did get in he made his way on to the pitch where he acted as an unofficial cheerleader. To the cheers of all the Midlands fans, he swung his foot at one of the footballs, only to see his shoe come flying off! It was a good job the fans had a sense of humour. "They would need one," said Nigel, "Peter Aldis was caught out when he put the ball past me into his own net late into the first-half (after thirty-two minutes). We couldn't put two passes together, it was dire, and we were just not in it at all for the first forty-five minutes. We were confident enough in the dressing room and thought we could get something out of the game. We knew Burnley should have been out of sight at half-time and the fact they weren't only gave us hope." Against the odds 'Packy' came good and equalised after sixty-four minutes. A move that he and Leslie Smith had been practising in training had paid dividends and Villa lived to fight another day. The replay was scheduled for four days' time, but it hadn't stopped raining in 'Brum' and the pitch was a mud bath. The referee, Mr Topliss from Grimsby, decided that the Villa's claret shirt would clash with the black kit that Burnley had bought down with them and if the Villa, who were the hosts, couldn't sort something out he would happily postpone the game. Villa would turn out for the replay in borrowed Birmingham City's red away shirts. 'Packy' played in the number eleven shirt that belonged to Alex Govan, City's pint-sized Glaswegian and outside-left. Every time McParland bent down the shirt would roll up his back like a window blind. The weather wasn't helping and Villa players were finding it hard to pick out the Burnley players. It was a wet, dark, filthy afternoon, in the days before Villa Park had floodlights, and Burnley's dark kit made them blend in against the dark background of the crowd. It would be a match remembered more for the stamina shown in these atrocious conditions on the pitch, rather than the skills on show. Many Burnley fans labelled the Villa players a dirty and tough bunch after the final whistle. "Sour grapes if you ask me" Nigel remembered, "After all, we just had dumped their team out of the Cup. Stan Lynn even got an anonymous, vicious pen letter from a small Lancashire town, the postmark; - Burnley!" But as bad as these conditions, the Villa supporters weren't fair-weather fans and over 46,000 hardy souls turned up to shout the boys on. Three close friends of Stan Crowther's were sacked from their factory jobs when they downed tools and made their way to Villa Park to watch the game. Stan wasn't concerned for their future, though. "They were all good lads and they got jobs the next day!" By the interval, team captain Johnny Dixon had given the home side a 1-0 advantage after winning a tussle with Burnley stopper Blacklaw; then Peter 'Mac' came along and did what he did best with a second goal. Nigel finished with his second clean sheet on the FA Cup trail and the Villa went on to beat their bogey team, Burnley, 2-0. From there, they progressed to a semi-final showdown. It would be with local rivals Birmingham, the Albion, or with Manchester United. This was the first time the three Midland sides had made the 'semis' in the same season. The wise money was on Manchester United to book one of the final Wembley places and they looked like odds-on favourite for taking the League Championship. Before their next League game was played, Villa would find out who would stand in their way of reaching a ninth FA Cup Final. The 'semis' would be played on

March 23rd, Aston Villa played West Bromwich Albion at Molineux, Wolverhampton and Manchester United played Birmingham at Hillsborough, Sheffield. Pretty good odds on an all-West Midlands final - which would be the first one since West Brom had beaten Birmingham City in 1931. Villa had also met Albion in the final, on three other occasions; overall, Villa lead that 2-1. Or might there be a supercharged Villa-Birmingham final? The only thing that was certain was the presence of a West Midlands' side at Wembley in May.

Villa now had just under a month to put some much-needed points on the board before their semi-final showdown. This started with a tough trip to Old Trafford, followed by two consecutive home fixtures. Aston Villa had started to play with a lot more poise and purpose; the consistently unchanged team sheet and their Cup victories had added continuously to their confidence. From mid-December the defence remained unchanged and Stan Crowther fitted in effortlessly to his accustomed wing-half role at the expense of the injured Baxter. The only change in the five-man forward-line was the number nine shirt, which alternated between Derek Pace and Billy Myerscough.

The trip to Manchester United was hugely satisfying; Man United had been six points clear at the top of the Division before the kick-off. They'd also turned around a 5-3 defeat away to Athletic Bilbao in Spain in the quarter-finals of the European Cup, by winning at home 3-0 to reach the semi-finals; just over a month ago. They were on fire, but the Villa boys held the leaders to a draw on their own patch. Villa had shown mettle to come back from a one-goal interval deficit with a goal from their captain, Dixon. Nigel knew how important it was to come out confident that day, "There was a good chance we would meet Matt Busby's boys in the final at Wembley, so the first thing we wanted to do was show them that we were not here to roll over, we were up for the fight. It looked likely they would retain their title and it would need a bloody good performance whichever team they come up against - that's assuming United reached the final - to stop them from taking the double."

The first of the Villa Park fixtures was Cardiff City who were in nineteenth place. Villa sent them back over the border, empty-handed, with a resounding 4-1 win. McParland and Sewell were among the scorers that day and that brought their tally to twenty goals between them. Three days later Arsenal came to town and went home after sharing the points in a 0-0 draw. That was Nigel's eleventh clean sheet of the campaign so far. After the game Villa were sitting in thirteenth position but they had four games in hand over many of the sides around them. With some headway made in the table, it was time to switch attention; Cup football was back on the agenda.

This was Aston Villa's first FA Cup Semi-Final since before the Second World War, when they had been a Second Division side for the only time in their history. There really was nothing to choose between the Villa and the Albion when they came together in the semi-final, with just three points separating them - West Brom in tenth place in the League compared to Villa's thirteenth position with a game in hand. Albion had scored forty-eight goals and conceded forty-four; the Villa had netted forty-four but had also leaked four fewer than Albion.

Both the 'Throstles' and the 'Villans' would go into the match sharing the record of appearing in the most FA Cup Semi-Finals, yet this was the first time they had squared up to each other in a 'semi;' each making their fifteenth showing at this stage, both having won nine and lost six. Villa had the slight upper-hand on their opponents by virtue of having lifted the famous trophy on six previous occasions to Albion's four. West Brom's last time just three years before. Seven of their victorious '54 side would play in this year's 'semi.' Neither team had to travel far from their respective grounds, but Birmingham would have to go north to Sheffield.

The Aston Villa team had remained unchanged for the previous six Cup ties, but now Derek Pace was injured. Billy Myerscough was given the nod to step in. Villa were confident, they'd been given 'insider information' from their centre-half Jimmy Dugdale, who had a history with West Brom and played with most of their lads in the 1954 Cup Final win. West Bromwich Albion certainly started the better team; they were one-up in less than two minutes, thanks to their inside-right, Brian Whitehouse, who unleashed an angled twenty-yard shot from the right-hand side after an intelligent ball from left-winger Roy Horobin. The ball flashed across the goalmouth, and as Nigel dived, the ball rolled under his huge frame before he was down completely. It was Villa who had an earlier chance, the ball finding Peter McParland on the left of the penalty area, he drove a vicious shot at goal, but the Albion 'keeper Jimmy Sanders was equal to it. Jimmy was quick to get rid of the ball and set up an Albion counter-attack in the face of Villa's Johnny Dixon who had closed in on him.

Villa kept the score down 'by the skin of their teeth.' Stan Lynn played a part and cleared one off the line, and then Nigel smothered a shot from Horobin. The West Brom forwards were described on the match newsreel as being a 'determined lot,' but Villa kept their heads and their coolness paid dividends when they were on the move for a lightning equaliser. Dixon sent the ball over, McParland put his head on it and the ball flew straight into the bottom corner of the net just out of Sanders reach. With seven minutes left of the half they were all-square. Wing-half Crowther took a shot from the edge of the area just as he slipped on the turf; the ball beat Jimmy Sanders but rattled the woodwork. Sanders was still on the floor when the ball, which was still in play came back with Dixon sliding in, the Albion centre-half Joe Kennedy managed to hook it away from danger. Then a minute before the interval, the normally reliable left-half, Pat Saward failed to clear a bouncing ball and gave Albion their second chance of the half, Whitehouse pouncing for his second. The 'Baggies' had looked the better of the two sides.

In the second-half the chances were few and far between, due to the hard and bumpy pitch. There were just five minutes remaining and it looked like the Villa's Cup journey had run its course. The referee was checking the time, when Myerscough who had drifted out to the wing, beat Don Howe, and centred the ball over for McParland to half-hit it, sending the ball bobbling towards the net. Len Millard tried in vain to keep it out. This was the second time the Irishman had cancelled out Whitehouse strikes and brought the 'Villans' level.

The game ended in a stalemate. Both sides knew before the forthcoming Thursday afternoon replay, which would be played at St Andrew's, that the winners of the tie would be down to play Busby's side at Wembley on May 4th. United had made light work of Birmingham in their 'semi' and the scoreline of 2-0 might have been substantially bigger.

When the Villa met their opponents for the replay, they lined-up with the same eleven that had done the job at Molineux. A stroke of fortune took the Albion's influential centre-forward Ronnie Allen out of play, following an accidental clash of heads with his former teammate and Villa centre-half Jimmy Dugdale. For the rest of the match, Dugdale was greeted with the crowd's displeasure every time he touched the ball; this was to be followed with the inevitable 'poison pen letters.' Ronnie knew there was nothing malicious in the tackle from his good friend, but that didn't help Jimmy's cause at the time.

That day at St Andrew's, Aston Villa led a charmed life. Albion's attack wasn't quite the same after Allen got 'nutted' which left West Brom with ten men. Myerscough put the Villa one-up in the first-half, when he managed to throw himself at a 'goalkeeper bound' McParland shot. His head reached it a fraction of a second before Jim Sanders could catch hold of it and Myerscough, who was by this time on his knees, watched the ball hit the back of the net. That all-important goal was only his fourth of the season.

Nigel was under increasing pressure as the second-half wore on. "They were desperate, the centre-half Kennedy came up and his header beat me, I couldn't do anything but watch the ball roll along the bar; it could have gone anywhere. Another attempt went begging; it was goal bound for definite, but Stan Lynn had his back to the ball as he was running towards the goal and he clipped the ball with his heel! We were lucky that day; we all went back to Villa Park after the game and celebrated in true style."

So Aston Villa had made it, they were to play in a record ninth FA Cup Final against formidable opponents, Matt Busby's Manchester United, in just over five weeks.

With a Wembley showdown booked, the Villa would have to knuckle down and finish their remaining League games. The Cup commitments had left them behind with eleven games still to be played and their feet needed to be put back firmly on the ground, Eric Houghton gave Nigel and the lads a team talk to remember for the first League game after the Albion victory. "Now lads, don't become too wrapped up with thoughts of Wembley and not getting injured. It's when you ease off that you are more likely to get caught!"

Preston North End were the first to be 'put to the sword' at Villa Park at the end of March. Myerscough and Sewell goals doing the damage and giving the 'Claret and Blues' both points in that 2-0 win, and moving Villa up into twelfth position; one point behind Newcastle United who had played thirty-seven games to Villa's thirty-two. Newcastle didn't have the distraction of Cup football after going out at Millwall in the fourth round. Fixture congestion was an understatement. Villa had to clear their backlog of League games before May 4th. There were still ten games to get through with only one month left in which to play them. Trips to Cardiff City and Chelsea brought a solitary point, with only three days between the two games. Sunderland were the visitors two days later. Pace and Myerscough were vying for the number nine shirt for the Cup Final and both would stake their claim by scoring a goal. Villa were on the move again, up to eleventh place, still games in hand over every team above them.

The schedule was heavy going and with just two days' break between games, Villa were at St Andrew's. Eric Houghton decided that he had to rest some of the first team. They were known throughout football, as being hardened, well-conditioned ninety-minute players but four games in eight days was a punishing timetable for anyone. Roy Chapman stepped up to the mark as a replacement for Jackie Sewell and scored two well-taken goals against the 'Blues.' In the following game at home to Sheffield Wednesday, Nigel was given the chance to rest and a young Arthur Sabin stepped in as his deputy.

"I had done a bit of work with Arthur. I would tell him in training when to come out for the ball, when to stay tall or when to go down. Even if his instincts told him otherwise, do what I say and if it goes wrong it is my fault. I will take the blame."

Arthur kept a clean sheet on his debut, as the Villa ran rings around their opponents, scoring a further three goals after first-half efforts from Sewell and Myerscough. The resulting 5-0 win pushed Villa up to tenth in the table and helped their goal average considerably.

Turf Moor was the next venue and the Villa sent an inexperienced defence up to Lancashire. Nigel, Stan Lynn, Peter Aldis and Stan Crowther were rested, their places being given to Michael Pinner, Dennis Jackson Roy Pritchard and Trevor Birch respectively. Villa went down to the odd goal 2-1, Pace scoring the only Villa goal. The next two fixtures would feature what would become the starting eleven for the Cup Final: Sims, Lynn, Aldis, Crowther, Dugdale, and Saward, Smith, Sewell, Myerscough, (who ultimately got the nod ahead of a desperately unlucky Pace) Dixon and McParland. This side would take maximum points against both Newcastle United with a 2-1 away win, and the Wolves at Villa Park with a 4-0 victory, scoring a total of six goals and conceding only one. This totalled to eight games in nineteen days and there were still two League games to go. Wolves at Molineux was the following day. Nigel was rested again, Michael Pinner being given his final Aston Villa run out, letting in three goals in a 3-0 defeat. Finally, the curtain fell on the League season on April the 27th. Luton were the visitors winning 3-1 in a match that no one really cared about. Nigel was glad to see it end, "Each and every one of the players was glad to see the back of that one. It was bloody ridiculous - we played ten games in one month! Why we couldn't play two or three after the Cup Final? I don't know. Anyway now we could look forward to our trip to London."

Aston Villa's season had finally finished. Tenth in the League and an FA Cup Final to be played, they would have settled for that at the beginning of the campaign!

CHAPTER FIVE

AGAINST ALL ODDS

With the League campaign finally finished for Aston Villa, the club could now turn their undivided attention to the FA Cup Final and how to beat Manchester United, the League winners for the last two seasons. United's successful defence of their 55/56 title meant that if they could beat the Villa on May 4th at Wembley, then they could wrest the title of 'double winners' from the Villa's grasp. Only Preston North End, in the League's inaugural season of 1888-89 and then Aston Villa in 1896-97 had ever achieved 'the double.' Aston Villa had it in their power to stop Manchester United from gatecrashing this exclusive club and if the Villa were successful they would also become the first side to hold aloft the Cup on seven occasions.

Busby's side had clinched the League title with three games to spare as far back as April 20th, with a resounding 4-0 win at home to Sunderland. Where Villa had no more distractions however, Manchester United still had the second leg of the European Cup Semi-Final against the mighty Spanish giants Real Madrid to come. They were chasing a 3-1 reversal from the first leg in the Santiago Bernabeu Stadium. They were still in contention until April 24th to collect three trophies, but by the following day this number had been reduced to two. Real were able to snatch a draw at Old Trafford and progressed on aggregate, 5-3, to get to their second of what became five consecutive European Cup Final victories.

Aston Villa's Wembley preparations were certainly more modest. Immediately after the semi-final victory a meeting was organised by centre-half Dugdale at Villa Park. The players had the backing of Eric Houghton and Bill Moore, the trainer, to capitalise on the fact they had reached the final and to make themselves a few bob out of it. Each player was allocated a job; some were to organise a dance to be held at the Gay Tower Ballroom in Edgbaston, a few organised boot sponsorship, with the manufacturer chucking £150 into the kitty. Swallow

Raincoats donated a free coat to every player after being approached by the captain Johnny Dixon. A good earning enterprise was the ASTON VILLA 'PREPARED', the official handbook of Aston Villa FC players, 1956-57. This gave the fans a little insight into their heroes' lives and brought them closer to the players. At the time it sold for one shilling and six pence and was a similar publication to the club's yearly annual. The local 'Sports Argus' paper drummed-up some real interest when it advertised the book, telling the fans that, 'a real life Aston Villa player will hand you your book - think of that!' But by far the biggest money-spinner for the players' pot was the allocation of one thousand tickets for the final. The majority of these were for the terracing; the ones near the Royal Box where the Queen would be in attendance were reserved mostly for family and close friends.

Training was changed to a different venue. "It was widely known that the Cadbury works at Bournville had a pitch that was the envy of some League teams. Honestly it was like a tennis court," Nigel recalled. "The finalists were granted permission to train on the pitch that was supposed to be similar to the Wembley turf, but after a couple of games on it, our trainer, Bill Moore, was worried that there were a few too many bumps on the surface and a player could go over on his ankle. The club arranged to take us up to Blackpool for the week; they thought the brisk seaside air would be of benefit to us. We stayed at the Norbreck Hotel. While we were staying there we had the British Heavyweight Boxing Champion, Jack London and his son Brian, who also won the same title as his Dad in '58, come over to the hotel to see the players. They lived locally, in Blackpool and they were good lads. They liked football and before they left they told us if we didn't win they would come back and give us all a good hiding! They were only joking, but we won anyway, just to be on the safe side! We did our training on ground to the rear of the hotel. It was just a case of keeping loose, really, and keeping our minds occupied. Between Bill Moore and Phil Hunt, the trainers, and Jimmy Easson and Jimmy Hogan, the coaches, we were superbly fit; we were all ninety-minute men."

The Villa party travelled down to the capital on Friday and stayed at the Hendon Hall Hotel in leafy North London. Eric Houghton had been in London the day before, attending the Football Writers Association's Annual Dinner. He had taken the midnight train back to Birmingham from Euston accompanied by sports journalist Peter Morris, a lifelong Aston Villa fan. During the journey Morris asked the Villa boss what he thought of all the press comments saying that Villa had no chance on Saturday. Houghton replied in his quiet way, "You know, we've got Manchester United worried more than they have us. They are expected to win, we are not, so… What have we to lose?"

As the momentous occasion approached, the Villa side had almost picked itself. Sims, Lynn, Aldis, Crowther, Dugdale and Saward had known that they would start, as did the wing partnerships of Smith and Sewell on the right side, Dixon and McParland on the left. The only place where there was any issue was who would wear the number nine shirt? Pace had started the season as centre-forward until he picked up an injury in late September. By the early New Year he was back in the fold and had played in all six of the Villa's Cup ties, until Billy Myerscough became the preference for the semi-final against the Albion. It would be 'Doc' Pace who would lose out again; Myerscough had done himself no harm in heading the winner in the replay with the Baggies.

The Manchester United starting line-up was settled with the exception of one place. Forward Dennis Viollett had been given plenty of time to recover from a thigh injury he had sustained earlier in the season and it looked promising that he would be one of the starting eleven. However at breakfast time on the morning of the game, Viollett came clean and told his manager that his old groin injury was causing some discomfort, and it might have proved too much during the game and impact on the outcome. Viollett didn't want to let his teammates down, so he took the decision to stand aside for youngster Bobby Charlton to deputise as the inside-forward. The only other item on the agenda to sort, prior to the big day was avoiding the clash of the teams' colours. In accordance with the FA ruling, both teams would have to change their kit. Manchester United opted for their all white strip with red piping on the jerseys' collar and cuffs. Villa would relive history and appear in blue shirts with claret stripes as they had in their first Cup Final victory back in 1887.

On the morning of their Wembley showdown, the Villa team were driven the short distance from their hotel to the ground. Nigel remembered the atmosphere that day, "There were Villa fans everywhere. When they saw us, they broke out smiling and singing and waving flags, they all looked really happy! When we got to Wembley, Manchester United had already arrived. We had drawn lots before, and got the 'lucky' North dressing room so we made our way to it. After getting our kit on and going through our own pre-match routines, Billy, our trainer, came up to me and put his arm around my shoulder. 'I want you and Stan to stick close to Johnny, so when we collect the Cup, the pair of you can carry him on your shoulders,' he said."

Just before Eric Houghton proudly led his charges out into the Wembley sunshine, he told his players 'Win this boys and I'll give you the town hall!'

The teams emerged from the tunnel and it was Villa who looked more relaxed, the players all had smiles on their faces; United, by contrast looked nervous. As they lined-up to be introduced to the Duke of Edinburgh, the 'Villans' waved to their friends and families up in the stand, and they certainly didn't look overawed. The teams were as follows:

Aston Villa	Manchester United
1 Sims	1 Wood
2 Lynn	2 Foulkes
3 Aldis	3 Byrne
4 Crowther	4 Colman
5 Dugdale	5 Blanchflower
6 Saward	6 Edwards
7 Smith	7 Berry
8 Sewell	8 Whelan
9 Myerscough	9 Taylor
10 Dixon	10 Charlton
11 McParland	11 Pegg

The pitch was likened to a palace lawn. Johnny Dixon spun the coin, won, and chose to play with what little wind there was. Manchester United were the youngest Cup Final team ever, but they started off like veterans. United' winger, Johnny Berry, beat his man and cut across to pass to Taylor, but he wasn't quick enough and Sims was able to dive at the forward's feet. Then Villa staged one of their lightning counter-attacks right into the Manchester area. Jackie Sewell crossed the ball from the right, Peter McParland ran on into the area and heading the ball that went straight to Ray Wood, the United' 'keeper who collected. McParland followed through and they clashed. Both players fell to the turf, Duncan Edwards was in the area and hovered over Villa's prone Irish forward, not impressed. Referee Frank Coultas called for the trainers. Wood appeared to be in a bad way and there were only six minutes on the clock. After a lot of activity in the Manchester box, the stretcher-bearers were called and took Wood off the pitch. The game then resumed with Peter 'Mac' rubbing his head. Jackie Blanchflower had put on the United' goalie's jersey, without tucking it into his 'knicks' and was wearing a borrowed cap from a nearby photographer. He looked like a player from the past. Manchester United had to reshuffle, Edwards dropped back to the centre-half spot leaving the United' midfield lacking. Villa dominated the game for long periods while United were down to ten men, Sewell dictating in the centre of the park. Crowther passed Charlton, then he skipped past Edwards but his shot was plucked safely out of the air by the United' stand-in 'keeper. Every time United's forwards got into the Villa area Nigel would race out collect and in the same movement release the ball to start a classic Villa counter.

In the last few minutes of the first-half Ray Wood returned to play, operating on the right-wing and then the whistle blew for the interval. No goals.

Aston Villa kicked-off the second-half with all to play for. Ray Wood didn't come back out and Blanchflower continued to deputise. In their first attack, the Villa's outside-left McParland cut in and connected with a deep cross from the right, heading the ball, but it struck the woodwork and the rebound was gathered by Blanchflower. Then Ray Wood returned to play on the right-wing. Now having eleven men on the field, Manchester United pressed more, but Nigel was equal to all they could throw at him. The best chance of the game fell to Myerscough when 'Packy' had picked him out with a slide rule pass, the number nine had hurried his shot and it flew wide; the striker threw up his arms in disgust. Every time McParland touched the ball that afternoon the crowd booed and jeered - the Manchester United fans were holding a grudge for his taking Wood out of the game. That grudge was about to intensify. Villa captain Dixon had taken a short pass from Smith on the right, he in turn hitting a low centre and it was McParland that would send an unstoppable header flying into the United' net. Stand-in Blanchflower could do nothing, and it was debatable whether the regular 'keeper would have fared any better. Only five minutes later a Dixon shot rifled against the bar and came flying back out, that man McParland was the first to react and had it sent back in with force goalbound!

Aston Villa had a two-goal cushion; Crowther had played out of his skin all afternoon. Maybe, Villa could pull it off. Perhaps Manchester weren't invincible after all.

Tommy Taylor saw a header pushed over by 'Nigger' Sims. The ball was crossed and again it was put out of 'harm's way' for another corner. Duncan Edwards took it from the left side and, as it went across the goalmouth, Taylor responded first, his head connected and the ball was in the top corner. With the deficit halved, United put Wood back in goal and they threw everything they could at the 'Claret and Blues,' but the Midlanders held firm; when the final whistle blew Aston Villa had seemingly done the impossible, won the FA Cup and denied Manchester United 'the double.' The Manchester fans couldn't believe that a squad of the Villa's calibre had beaten their side.

Johnny Dixon was an incredibly proud man, leading his troops in battle to victory, now he was leading them up the steps to be presented to the Queen, and awarded their victory spoils - the FA Cup! First Johnny Dixon as captain, would hold aloft the trophy for Aston Villa. The last Villa captain to do likewise, had been Andy Ducat back in 1920. Dixon was followed by Sewell, Smith and Saward, then Stan Lynn, Aldis and centre-half Dugdale, close on his heels came Myerscough, scorer McParland and then Nigel Sims. Last but by no means least came wing-half Stan Crowther who had played an absolute blinder. They all followed their leader and claimed their 'gold.'

"Eric Houghton, barely two hours ago, had promised us the Town Hall, if we lifted the Cup. We didn't get that, but we did get £50 each!"

Had Blanchflower not been nominated 'Man of the Match' through circumstance, then Stan Crowther would surely have claimed the title that day. Aston Villa were record seven times FA Cup winners! Immediately the press went into overdrive writing stories, and disparaging Aston Villa's achievement. They had done this since Villa had put Burnley out in the sixth round. The headline theme being; had the Albion not lost Ronnie Allen, Villa wouldn't have progressed - an 'old chestnut' well past its sell by date! Now the press could get their teeth into Wood's early return to the dressing room, through injury, it was as though, Villa had cheated or stolen the Cup from Manchester United. Nigel wasn't bothered in the slightest, "You have to take what life throws at you; Aston Villa did. We didn't fear United like a lot of teams did, we played our game and it paid off. We were the better team and even if Ray had been okay for the entire game we would still be going up to lift that Cup!"

The official party made their way across the capital for the celebration dinner held at the Grosvenor Hotel. "It was quite a party, once all the speeches were out of the way and it lasted well into the small hours," was all Nigel would say, smiling.

Club President Sir Patrick Hannon mentioned in the course of his after dinner speech that the winning of the trophy had been a thirty-year ambition of his and it had now been realised. Other speakers included the Chairman of the Football Association, the Lord Mayor of Birmingham and Villa Director, Norman Smith.

The famous trophy, 'on its way back home,' would travel with the club by rail on the Sunday afternoon. Huge crowds greeted the Cup and the team as they emerged from Birmingham's Snow Hill station. A coach relayed the team to the Birmingham Council House for the civic reception laid on by the proud city.

As the sun went down, Aston Villa Football Club were greeted by thousands upon thousands of their fans lining the streets all the way from the city centre to Aston. En-route down

Corporation Street the Central Fire Station had opened its doors and in a row outside were the station fire engines. The firemen saluted by ringing their appliance bells as the Aston Villa side passed on their way, to place the famous trophy at Villa Park for the next twelve months.

"That was one of the most memorable days I ever had. Coming in to Birmingham along the road in that coach, there must have been millions - there were 250,000 people in the square (in front of Birmingham Council House) - unbelievable isn't it! I was a 'nobody,' but not now! I had won the Cup."

The club opened the stadium for the masses that had waited, some for many hours, and, as a show of appreciation, Johnny Dixon and Les Smith walked around the pitch to huge cheering. The players disappeared from view for a while, but then turned up in the Directors' Box. The police couldn't contain the fans that charged from the terracing, across the pitch and cheered the players as they all took turns in holding aloft the 'pot.' The trainer, manager and then the Chairman all had a turn. The crowd then turned their attentions calling for 'Doc' Pace who had missed the final. Derek's appearance raised the loudest cheer of the afternoon. Jackie Sewell said "Villa appealed to the Football Association for Pace to receive a medal. They were given permission and Villa had a medal struck up for the 'Doc'."

The following week a banquet, hosted by Birmingham's newspapers, was held for Aston Villa's team of Champions at the Grand Hotel in Birmingham. Captain Johnny Dixon was called on to say a few words. He spoke hesitantly and very quietly, choked and close to tears, as he told the audience of just what this achievement had meant for the players, the club and to the supporters. "How lucky we are to have such loyal supporters; they were perhaps more confident than us that we would bring this Cup back!" The mutual trust and respect among his troops was touched on too. Included in the invited guests and listening to the speeches were famous names from Villa's glorious FA Cup past. Sam Hardy - possibly the last great Villa 'keeper, and a Cup winner in 1913 and 1920. His fellow teammates from the 1913 victory - skipper Joe Bache and Harry Hampton (who scored both goals in the Villa's 1905 victory). Others present representing the 1920 success were, Frank Barson, Charlie Wallace, Tommy Smart and scorer Billy Kirton. Tommy and Billy had the misfortune to be on the losing 1924 side, as did Dickie York who was also a guest at the banquet. The 1924 FA Cup Final was only the second time the Wembley Empire stadium had hosted this event. The most notable guest of the evening was the last surviving team member of the 1897 Aston Villa 'double' winning side, left-back Albert Evans.

Special notice was given to remembering the former Villa Chairman the late Frederick Normansell. Fred, a local councillor, had been Chairman of the club for nearly two decades, up until his death in 1955 and was known as a caring, popular and highly respected gentleman.

CHAPTER SIX

BREAD AND BUTTER DAYS

Aston Villa Football Club was firmly back in the spotlight and at the forefront of Association Football. They had rewritten history, now that a team had lifted the most famous trophy in world football for a seventh time. The legendary players of Villa's halcyon days would surely be proud if they could see their club's latest achievement. Had the 'slumbering giant' finally woken?

As Cup winners, Aston Villa found themselves invited to play in some real 'money spinning' games. They were set to play a series of exhibition matches in Germany and also had an invitation to play the mighty Real Madrid in the Spaniard's stadium. "Eric Houghton didn't want us going over to Spain, he said it would tire us out," but Nigel and his teammates were more than willing to go. "We could have put up with it; we didn't mind being tired one bit. We would have collected £300 per man to face Real and in those days that was a serious amount of money - it was nearly three months wages."

The traditional Charity Shield game between the League Champions and the FA Cup Winners would be played later in the season, and it would be a rematch against Busby's lot. As the English Cup holders, Aston Villa accepted an invitation to play their French counterparts Toulouse, who were winners of the Coupe de France after defeating SCO Angers 6-3 on May 23rd in the Stade Olympique, Yves-du-Manoir. Villa's post-season was arranged. The team flew out to Germany on May 12th, with a few of the official party choosing to go by sea. They took in two scheduled matches in Germany, returned to the United Kingdom and then finished their tour playing in France. Villa played against HSV Hamburg on May 18th and then FSV Frankfurt on May 21st. The starting eleven for the first match was:

Sims, Lynn, Aldis, Crowther, Dugdale, Birch, Smith, Sewell, Myerscough, Dixon, McParland

Villa defeated Hamburg 3-1 with McParland, Sewell and Dixon scoring. It was all the more remarkable for Aston Villa, as their German hosts had been the losing finalists in the 1956 DFB - Pokal Final, the German equivalent of the FA Cup, and runners-up in the previous League campaign (1956-57) of the German Bundesliga. Hamburg would go on to be the runners-up again in the following 58/59 season.

Nigel remembered an incident at a reception after the Hamburg game. "We were at a civic banquet type thing and McParland and the German team's 'keeper bumped into one another accidentally at the bar. 'Packy' later told me that the German, in broken English, had called him a 'goalkeeper killer.' He was referring to the Ray Wood incident back in the May Cup Final, the players later learned that it had been screened all over Europe.

The next day, the Villa made a very early start, and took the five-hundred-kilometre rail journey south for the Frankfurt game. The line-up was the same, with the exception of Birch, who was replaced by Saward. Pat Saward had been delayed after selection for the Republic of Ireland side in their World Cup qualifier against England in Dublin. Villa gained their second victory with an identical scoreline, defeating FSV Frankfurt. After half an hour Sewell had to step down with Pace deputising. Sewell came back on again later in the match, taking over from Pace. Sewell, Dixon and McParland notched Villa's goals. "There was quite a 'to do' at the end of the match. Eric Houghton had told the Frankfurt officials that we wouldn't play under floodlights under any circumstances. We were somewhat surprised when the lights went on with probably ten minutes remaining. Eric was livid in the dressing room, but being the gent he was, he didn't take his protest further."

"It took us over ten hours by train, followed by the most

horrendous channel crossing I have ever had the misfortune to experience before we got back home. Honestly it was the longest two hours of my life and it was a relief to get back on dry land! The Villa board expected us to do the same again as we had to go to France the following week to play the French Cup Winners. I think it was 'Packy' who made our feelings known. We were sick to death of trains and boats. The board relented and we ended up flying to Paris."

The Villa party flew to Paris from Elmdon Airport, on Tuesday May28th. The clash of the respective Cup winners, Aston Villa representing England versus Toulouse de Francais was played the following day in the Parc de Princes, Paris. Thanks to the good old English press Villa were seen to be 'proper villains' with a tarnished reputation, which first surfaced in the early Cup rounds. It turned out that the Toulouse players were on the equivalent of £40 per man to 'put one over' the Villa, and they did… literally! It was ironic that the Villa fielded the same team that had lined-up at Wembley's twin towers barely three weeks previously. Villa lost the game 2-1, with captain Johnny Dixon getting the goal - he scored in every tour match. Nigel did not remember the match fondly. "They were dirty so and so's, I don't think they were all French, possibly some Algerians or perhaps Moroccans. Anyway the only friendly contact was when Johnny shook hands with their captain. It was 'gloves off' as soon as the whistle went. They were kicking at head height and I am over six feet tall, pulling shirts, they spat at us, they were horrible little men. The police were called on to the pitch to drag their trainer off and to stop the fighting going on between their players and our centre-half Jimmy Dugdale. Jimmy was a huge lad, he just stood there watching it all, the fans were hissing and booing, so what did he do? He bowed at them. They went absolutely mad, the place just erupted."

Jackie Sewell the Villa's inside-right remembered the Paris

incident. "It wasn't good; at least Jimmy had a sense of humour, though there were plenty of comedy moments. I remember a training session before the start of the campaign. We would often be taken out into the countryside for long runs along quiet country lanes and this one day we were driven to some golf club up near little Les Smith's neck of the woods (Halesowen). We got changed and after running five miles or so we turned and started heading back. I was up near the front when one of the lads said someone had fallen. Turning round and going back fifty yards or so we saw Nigel laid on this hedge. He hadn't fallen, he was having a rest! Nigel wasn't one for running. He could put himself about in the box, but he didn't run. Anyway Les Smith told the group to go on, said he would run back with Nigel. We all got back to within sight of the clubhouse, tongues hanging out and there, sitting on the clubhouse veranda, were Les and Nigel, with drinks in their hands. Smithy, the crafty little dog, had taken Nigel on a shortcut! Les was familiar with the area, see, and they had beaten us back by miles and hadn't even broken sweat. Les and Nigel were the closest of mates I ever saw in my time in football, one six-foot odd and the other five-foot odd! They had both come to Villa from the same team, Wolves."

Surprisingly a more relaxed atmosphere than they had encountered in Paris, greeted the 'Claret and Blues' in the opening fixture of the 57/58 campaign, and that was an away game against Birmingham City! The starting eleven was the same lads who had taken to the Wembley pitch just three months before. 50,780 fans packed into St Andrews but by the interval Villa trailed by the odd goal. When the final whistle blew they had lost by a bigger margin, but at least 'Packy' had opened his account in the 3-1 reversal. Then a home win and both points at the expense of Raich Carter's Leeds United were most welcome. It was obvious from the kick-off that Leeds had come down from Yorkshire with the intention of shutting the Villa out at all costs, especially after their opening day 3-0 defeat at Blackpool. Leeds failed in their bid to stop the Midlanders from scoring twice and even though they were unable to find the net themselves, they were still able to inflict their own style of damage on the Villa. On thirty minutes, Les Smith went off to receive stitches for a bad gash below his knee - and it was just a question of when, not if, the next Villa lad would suffer a similar fate. Jimmy Dugdale duly obliged and was the next casualty to trot off, late in the second-half, with a badly cut eye. With three stitches inserted, Jimmy was soon back at centre-half. Nigel remembered how keen they were to put 'one in' as well as put 'one over' the Villa. "They tried all they could to intimidate us; they weren't happy to see Dugdale come back on, and they could see that we would give as good as we got. They tried it on a few times with me but saw they would get short shrift and I was too big to mess with." Immediately following this bad tempered game Aston Villa went down 1-0 in a home defeat at the hands of Everton. Leslie Smith had to sit this and the next game out. He only got played in the following two fixtures before disaster struck and he broke his collarbone in a 2-0 victory at home to Luton Town. This inconsistent team pattern would follow continue until the end of September. The only notable result was a 5-1 mauling of newly-promoted Second Division Champions, Leicester City; Sewell was amongst the scorers with a brace and Peter McParland scored for his fifth game running. The 'Foxes' were finding it difficult in the top-flight and, after the Villa game finished; they were rooted firmly at the foot of the table. Other September events worthy of mention apart from the 'Villans' two wins, were the call up for Villa wing-half Stan Crowther to play for England Under-23's against their Bulgarian counterparts in London the following Wednesday. Also, at the clubs eighty-second Annual General Meeting, Aston Villa would nominate a fourth Club Vice-President, Mr Walter Lewis CBE; a former Mayor of Birmingham, who took his place alongside the other Vice-Presidents.

October was a horrendous month for the 'Villans', as they lost four out of their five League fixtures. They conceded four goals in each of the first three games; faring slightly better in each of the remaining two games, letting only three into the net. Arsenal, Manchester United and Chelsea did most damage. Villa's only win that month was a close 4-3 home victory over Newcastle. To make matters worse, Villa's highly respected trainer Bill Moore left - he was sacked after a disagreement with the board. Houghton, out of loyalty to his close friend, came close to severing his ties with the club. Bill had been the trainer at Notts County under Eric and had followed the manager across the Midlands in '53, when Houghton took the Aston Villa job.

As winners of the Cup Final in May, the Villa had qualified to play in the Charity Shield, an annual fixture that set the Cup Winners against the Division One Champions. The match was staged at Old Trafford and would go down in history as the first game Villa had played under floodlights. At Eric Houghton's suggestion both Peter McParland and Ray Wood were made captains for the evening, the idea being to sweep aside any ill feeling toward the Villa's Irishman and to keep the 'boo boys' silent after the FA Cup Final incident. The press had been hanging on to it since May, and it was becoming a witch-hunt. Although the game was played on the Red's turf, it didn't give Manchester United their 'normal' home advantage. The fans didn't seem quite as enthusiastic for this fixture as they had for the visit of the Villa only a fortnight earlier. That game had pulled in a 43,332 crowd to witness Villa's first capitulation; with Pace scoring the Villa's consolation goal in a 4-1 drubbing. A crowd of less than 28,000, turned out for the exhibition match. During the game Manchester United's wing-half Duncan Edwards slid in on Jackie Sewell to regain possession of the ball. Wrapping both of his legs round Sewell's right leg, Edwards twisted then jerked his whole body and Jackie was convinced he'd just had his leg broken. While the Villa inside-forward sat on the turf surveying the damage to his leg, Edwards bent down and said, "That's for Wembley!" Sadly Edwards was one of the lads who perished in the Munich air disaster, "I remember Duncan," said Stan Crowther, "he was a quality player, though he just never turned it on when he faced me." For the next three games Jackie Sewell was out. It couldn't be said Villa emerged with their heads held high, but they did emerge with a silver plaque presented to the team by the Mayor of Stretford.

The month couldn't end quickly enough. Villa had shipped a dozen goals more than they had scored and they were sitting with only three sides under them in the League table. Nigel was clearly unhappy; he had picked the ball out of the net more times than he cared to remember, and only two clean sheets was nothing to crow about. "We just didn't know what was going to happen from one game to the next. We were playing our same game week in week out, sometimes we could punish teams by hitting four or five goals; then in other games we would be on the receiving end, and that's not a nice feeling. I can't recall picking the ball out of the net so often in games yet I got a call up to represent the Football League Eleven." (Nigel played in the match against the League of Ireland at Elland Road on October 9th) Jimmy Dugdale also had the distinction of representing the Football League at Old Trafford against an Army XI opposition. November had a brighter start. Villa maintained a 2-1 interval lead against Portsmouth, with strikes by Tommy Southren, who stood in for the injured Sewell, and one from the ever-reliable 'Doc' Pace.

Nigel insisted on playing in the next game at the Hawthorns, even though he was carrying a shoulder injury, but was powerless to prevent the 3-2 defeat. The only bright notes of the day were young Walter Hazleden being blooded against the

'Baggies,' becoming the youngest player ever to appear for the Villa and scoring, too. Some debut! The other was Stan Crowther notching up his first strike. Things didn't improve for Nigel; his shoulder injury worsened during the week and that meant he had to sit out when 'Spurs' visited Villa Park.

As a result of Nigel's injury Arthur Sabin was told he would be starting his second match, filling him with excitement. "He was a really likeable lad. We had watched him quietly turning in some very good performances for the second string and in training and we knew he could be relied upon to do well if called in. I used to say that I would have to stay on top of my game, because 'once I go off,' Sabin will walk straight into my place!" Nigel said.

"He was close to Stan, with both of them being just youngsters." Jackie Sewell was referring to wing-half Stan Crowther. Sewell came back for his first game since being crocked in the Charity Shield and scored the Villa goal in the 1-1 draw with Tottenham. The result ensured both teams remained as they were before kick-off. 'Spurs' sat in thirteenth place while Villa were having a harder time of it down in nineteenth. They were like the Villa of old, and their inability to score kept them in the lower reaches. Leicester City were bottom yet they had scored five goals more than the Villa.

The next game was a trip to The City Ground on the banks of the River Trent. Nottingham Forest had made a good solid start under the leadership of Billy Walker and went into fifth position at the close of play after mauling Villa 4-1. Forest had been one-up after only four minutes but a smartly taken individual goal by Crowther, lobbing the 'keeper, had brought the 'Claret and Blues' level. Villa were now only one point above Sheffield Wednesday, who occupied one of the relegation spaces, but Wednesday had a game in hand.

December came bringing an improvement. The 'Villans'

were comfortably 3-0 up at half-time against fellow strugglers Sheffield Wednesday and they added another two in the second-half, to defeat the 'Owls' a convincing 5-2. Hazleden and Crowther added two apiece with the more recognised scorer McParland bagging one. Crowther had only scored twice before in his time at the Villa, and the two he scored against the Sheffield side were to be his last; all his goals coming in a five-match spell. Vic Crowe started this, his fourth game of the season, having been gradually introduced in September. Now nearing full fitness, he played three games on the trot, then sat out two, before cementing the wing-half number four position as his own for the rest of the season.

A welcome distraction for the Villa supporters was the draw for the third round of the FA Cup when the 'big boys' come into the reckoning. This was made on Monday 8th December. Aston Villa would start their defence of the Cup with an away trip to the Potteries. The 'Villans' fluctuating League fortunes continued and another home defeat against Manchester City followed. Derek Pace played his last game in 'Claret and Blue' against City, before being lured by Joe Mercer to play for Sheffield United. He cost the 'Blades' £12,000.

As 1957 drew to a close, Aston Villa knew they were struggling to get goals and only 'Packy' had reached double figures. These desperate times required drastic action. Aston Villa turned their sights to a youngster plying his trade in Cardiff for the 'Bluebirds.' In his last campaign, this bustling forward had notched twenty-five goals in only forty-six appearances, an impressive strike rate. The Villa might have signed the lad back in '54, when he had been scoring goals for fun at Southern League Kidderminster Harriers, but for unknown reasons, Villa boss Houghton didn't want to pay the £1,500 asked for his services. The player in question was Gerry Hitchens. Before the Villa signed the Staffordshire-born player, they made enquiries to

Sunderland for Charlie Fleming. Villa had offered £11,000, but Sunderland rejected the bid. There was no room for negotiating, as it was more than fair for someone who at the age of thirty was getting on in their career. So the Villa turned their attention to Hitchens, completing the deal and making him Cardiff City's most expensive export. Houghton paid a considerable fee, much more than the Kidderminster side would have had settled for! It took a cool £22,500 to acquire Gerry's signature, and this huge fee was the club's fourth most-expensive transfer signing. A minor complication to the deal was that Hitchens had just started his National Service in the summer and still had a year and a half to serve before he could train full-time. From his signing on December 20th, Gerry had to wait just one day before he pulled on the famous 'Claret and Blue' number nine shirt against local rivals Birmingham City, with a crowd of 41,118 turning out to take a look. Unfortunately, the new signing didn't have the fairy tale start the fans were hoping for and couldn't find the net in the 2-0 defeat. Birmingham took the 'Second City' bragging rights back to Small Heath and recorded their first 'double' over their famous neighbours since the 1905/06 season.

Then suddenly bang, bang, bang! Three games, three wins and three Hitchens' goals. He might not have scored on his debut, but in his second appearance, he certainly hit the ground running. A 3-0 victory at home to Arsenal, with Stan Lynn weighing in with one, an unfortunate own goal, and then Hitchens, sending the 38,000 plus crowd home more than happy. In his next game Hitchens knocked in a double, one in each half on Merseyside to take the points from Everton - revenge for the defeat at Villa Park earlier in the season.

After missing the 'Spurs' game, Nigel had come straight back into the side to enjoy a run of seven League games. "We were starting to get it together more defensively and letting fewer goals creep in. We conceded nine in six games, that was going in the right direction. With Hitchens scoring at the other end we were expecting to climb the table and to go a long way to keeping our grasp firmly on 'our' trophy." Morale was good and two League wins had pushed Villa one place and three points away from the drop zone. Time to defend the FA Cup.

Aston Villa arrived at Second Division Stoke City at the beginning of January for their first game of 1958 and to start defending their Cup title. Villa, followed by a large number from the Midlands, swelling the crowd to 45,800, couldn't maintain their narrow interval lead given to them by the Wembley hero McParland. Conceding an equaliser they finished 1-1, and it was back to Villa Park to start all over again. The replay was staged the following Wednesday afternoon, a 2pm kick-off due to Villa Park not having floodlights at this time. Villa made two changes from the first match - Crowe replaced Crowther at wing-half and Hitchens got the nod over Billy Myerscough. Villa went in 2-1 down at the interval, Sewell being on target. Stan 'the wham' Lynn, another Cup Final winner, scored for Villa in the second-half, to add to new boy Hitchens' first Cup goal for his new side. The game ended all-square 3-3. Extra-time didn't provide a winner, so it was off to Molineux the following Monday for the third tie of the third round. This was Aston Villa's third game in only six days, a heavy schedule. Dugdale was replaced by Saward, with Crowther dropping into a more unaccustomed role at left-half. Here after a 0-0 half-time score, the Villa couldn't capitalise on the situation, but Stoke did; and with City scoring two goals, Villa's defence of the FA Cup came to an end. Just short of 122,500 fans had paid to watch this Cup marathon to its conclusion. "We were really gutted to have given up the trophy so easily, no disrespect to Stoke but they were Second Division, had we progressed, we would have faced another team from that Division in Middlesborough," Nigel said.

The first League game of the New Year had fallen between

the Stoke replays. Villa had been on fire that day hitting the north-eastern lads, Sunderland, for five. Hitchens didn't find the net, and it was left to Stan Lynn, the full-back, to show the others the way with a hat-trick, including two penalties. Villa would find their form become inconsistent once again, as they embarked on a sequence of four games without a win, conceding thirteen goals and notching up only three in reply. The worst result was a humiliating 6-1 beating by new boys Leicester City, who were still sitting dangerously close to the drop. Stan Crowther played at right-wing, in what would be his last appearance in 'Claret and Blue.' Vic Crowe switched wings, playing in place of Saward.

The season continued: On February 1st, Sheffield Wednesday were bottom of the pile having collected only eighteen points from twenty-eight games played. Above them were Sunderland, Leicester and Newcastle all on twenty-one points, Newcastle having played one game fewer than the other two sides. Leeds were on twenty-three points, then Villa, in seventeenth place, with Pompey one above, both sides again on twenty-three points, having played twenty-nine games apiece. Then came terrible news. On February 6th 1958 the Manchester United team plane crashed in Munich on the way back from a European game in Belgrade. Among the many fatalities were eight members of the 'Busby Babes' side. Nigel was stunned, "Utter disbelief, that's the only way I can describe it when I heard on the radio what had happened. Last May we played against them at Wembley. It was only nine months ago."

The Villa team attended the funeral of local born Duncan Edwards from Dudley. He was buried alongside his little sister Carol Anne who had died in 1947 at the age of only fourteen weeks.

In 2008, Nigel Sims, and a host of other star players from that era paid their respects and attended the fiftieth anniversary of the Munich disaster and in particular the loss of Edwards' life. "Derek Kevan the West Bromwich Albion centre-forward and myself were among others invited to attend the 'Fifty Years on' memorial service of Duncan Edwards taking place in Dudley. We were put up in a hotel in Brierley Hill the night before. The following morning as we made our way up to the church for the service, the press had been out in numbers, stopping any footballers they had seen and asked questions about Duncan. "Did he ever score against you Nigel?" One reporter asked me. "He wasn't that good," I replied jokingly.

A few weeks later Crowther stunned his teammates by leaving Villa for Manchester United. He had broken into the first team only in late September of the previous season. "Stan told me a few days after we had heard the news, how he had been taken up to Manchester by our boss Houghton. He hadn't expected to be doing anything other than watch a game with Eric. Instead he was introduced to Busby's right-hand man Jimmy Murphy, signed for them (United) and less than an hour later was playing for them against Sheffield Wednesday in a League match. The game was played only thirteen days after the crash, and they only just managed to assemble a side." The matchday programme for the game had a blank space where the Manchester United team should have appeared, such was the uncertainty.

Appearing for the Villa against Stoke City meant Stan was Cup-tied, but due to Manchester United's predicament, the Football Association granted them special dispensation and they were able to field Crowther in their Cup matches. Stan earned a runners-up medal in United's defeat by Bolton Wanderers in the '58 final. When he signed for Manchester United Busby was still hospitalised in Germany.

"When I did finally meet Busby, his first words to me were, "You're not my kind of player Crowther." The second time he spoke to me was in his office where another chap was sitting with his back to the door. It was the Chelsea manager Ted Drake. Busby told me I was off to Chelsea. I was dismayed." Stan Crowther was not a fan of Red's legend Matt Busby; nor it later emerged, of the world of football and he turned his back on the game altogether at the peak of his career, when aged just twenty-six.

Spring saw Aston Villa pick up four valuable points at Villa Park in their first two March fixtures. This did their goal average the world of good as they scored seven and conceded only two. Peter 'Mac' added two to full-back Lynn's contribution in a 3-0 win over Burnley. Then the winning streak was stopped in its tracks. Villa went down by one goal at Fratton Park and then were caned 6-2 at 'Spurs.' Nigel bent down so much that day at White Hart Lane he could have sustained a back injury!

When Manchester United came to town it should have guaranteed a good gate, but the paying public seemed to have lost all faith in the 'Villans', and only 16,631 bothered to show up. It served the ones that stayed at home right, as they missed Aston Villa's best display for a long while! With the United woodwork rattled twice in the first seven minutes, the Villa meant business. United took the lead against the run of play, but were drawn back all-square within twenty minutes. It was level pegging at half-time, with Myerscough having found the net for the home side. Villa came out after the interval with all guns blazing. Their persistence paid off when Hitchens, who now played at inside-right, hit home from twelve yards out. Nigel and his defence were then subjected to a late bombardment by Manchester United, finally conceding when the unmarked Dawson struck for the Reds. But the game was far from over and with a minute remaining, neat work between Smith, McParland and then Saward resulted in the ball finding Sewell who flicked it past United 'keeper Gregg, completing a 3-2 victory. Nigel was a

Coton in the Elms, a sleepy
village in Derbyshire.

A typical village scene in
Coton.

Nigel's childhood home and Nigel's parents Jack and Edith with (left) family
friend Mrs Case

Nigel aged seventeen at Wolves in 1948. Nigel appears on 49/50 autograph sheet.

Fellow lodger and good friend of Nigel's Johnny Walker. They remain close pals.

National Service: Nigel playing for Western Command at Anfield.

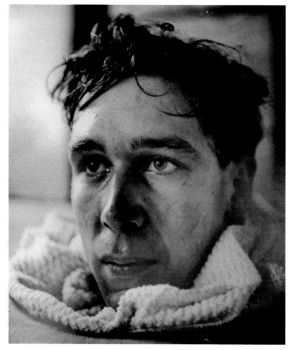

Hot under the collar – Wolves 1952.

A programme cover from
Wolves Division One
Championship year, their
first-ever.

WOLVERHAMPTON WANDERERS 1953/54
Back Row: J.Taylor, R.Flowers, B.Williams, R.Chatham, L.Gibbons, N.Sims, W.Slater, W.Wright.
Middle Row: J.Gardiner (Trn), J.Hancocks, R.Swinbourne, W.Shorthouse, J.Short, D.Wilshaw, J.Mullen, S.Cullis (Mgr).
Front Row: R.Pritchard, L.Smith, R.Stockin.

Nigel in the 1953/4 Wolves line up, they would go on to win the League.

Sightseeing in Moscow with Wolves teammates and (below) lining-up with teammates in Moscow 1955.

Above left: England XI v Young England XI Eve of Cup Final Programme 30 April 1954.

Nigel in his civvies and right and below in kit.

Above right: Arthur Sabin makes his debut for Villa v Sheffield
Wednesday April 1957. Villa won 5-0.

Aston Villa team travel '57 style.

Nigel and teammates see why Les Smith stuck with football 1957.

1957 FA Cup 6th Round. Villa won the replay 2-0.

1957 FA Cup Semi-Final v WBA
Nigel Sims versus Derek Kevan.

Nigel in action.

All photos are from the FA Cup Semi-Final replay win v WBA at St Andrews.
Nigel keeps a clean sheet in a 1-0 victory
1957, Wembley here we come!

Top: Team line-up with Wembley shirts.
Middle: The team reading good luck telegrams at Villa Park.
Bottom: Advert for the players' handbook... Cup Final ticket... Cover of Cup Final programme.

WEMBLEY 1957: Eric Houghton leads his men out/Nigel up against Tommy
Taylor/Just wide of the mark/Team on pitch thanking the fans/Nigel
denies Manchester United by pushing the ball over the bar.

Top: Trainer Billy Moore, Peter McParland and Nigel.
Bottom: (left) Chairing captain Johnny Dixon (right) Dressing room
celebrations.

On the bus to Villa Park parading the trophy. From left: Nigel, Peter McParland, Billy Myerscough, Jackie Sewell, Johnny Dixon and Stan Lynn.

Nigel with the FA Cup. Right Aston Villa versus French Cup Winners Toulouse at the Parc de Princes, Paris, 29 May 1957.

As always Nigel is in the thick of it.

Nigel keeps Chelsea at bay in a League game at Stamford Bridge 12 October 1957.

Arthur Sabin's funeral March 1958.

A happier occasion as Nigel becomes the first-ever Terrace Trophy winner in 1958.

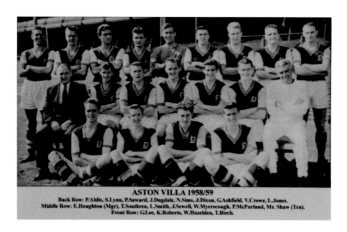

ASTON VILLA 1958/59
Back Row: P.Aldis, S.Lynn, P.Saward, J.Dugdale, N.Sims, J.Dixon, G.Ashfield, V.Crowe, L.Jones.
Middle Row: E.Houghton (Mgr), T.Southren, L.Smith, J.Sewell, W.Myerscough, P.McParland, Mr. Shaw (Trn).
Front Row: G.Lee, K.Roberts, W.Hazelden, T.Birch.

Nigel in action.

Celebrating victory at Burnley in the FA Cup 6th round replay 3 March 1959.

Nigel in action at Goodison Park 28 March 1959.
Unfortunately Villa lost 2-1.

Summer 1959: On tour with Arsenal against Juventus. Left: The great John Charles challenges Nigel for the ball. Right: John's brother Mel helps Nigel out in defence.

happy chap. "That gave us huge satisfaction; they beat us twice earlier in the season, but it was in that arrogant fashion they did it, that stuck in the craw, we certainly upset them lifting the Cup, at their expense."

For the second time that season there was sad news to come. On March 15th 1958, 'The Villa News & Record' reported that Arthur Sabin, the youngster who had featured in only two matches for the First eleven had died on Wednesday March 5th at Birmingham's Queen Elizabeth Hospital. The nineteen-year-old had suffered kidney problems. His last outing for the Villa was a Central League game at Villa Park against Barnsley on December 28th 1957. Nigel and his teammates, the Chairman, Directors and many club staff were among a large attendance at the funeral service at Aston Parish Church paying tribute to a player who showed every promise of making a great name for himself in the profession he loved so much. "All the lads went to the funeral, and Johnny Dixon, Jimmy Dugdale, Stan Lynn, Peter Aldis, Dennis Jackson and Roly Morris acted as coffin bearers. It was such a sad day, such a terrible waste of a short life. We all felt for the family and the youngster. He had played well all season for the Central League outfit. I know all the Villa coaching staff were expecting him to go on and make a name for himself. Some reporters were saying he was good enough to go on and play for England. He would ask my advice and he would use it to better himself. Arthur would hang on my every word, it was a crying shame." In a Birmingham paper after the funeral, a little piece was included from John Morrall of Bentley Heath, Solihull: 'My memory of Arthur Sabin's Villa Park debut concerns a man who stood in the same area of the ground as I did. He always shouted out 'Come on the Cat!' whenever big Nigel Sims touched the ball. The first time Arthur (who was considerably smaller than big Nigel) touched the ball, the cry was, 'Come on the Kitten!'."

In April the Villa went north to Lancashire to play Bolton Wanderers. Bolton had recently booked their place in the FA Cup Final when they defeated their arch rivals, Blackburn Rovers, in the semi-final. Bolton were sitting mid-table, but had played a game more than Villa, who were seven places lower in twentieth position. There were just seven points separating them, and the Villa had scored more goals then the 'Trotters.' Bolton won this one-sided contest 4-0. In the return fixture just four days later, Villa took their revenge by hitting Bolton with exactly the same 4-0 scoreline. Full-back Lynn scored a goal to take his tally to nine for the season. This was the Villa's second win in three days after turning over West Bromwich Albion 2-1 at Villa Park, thanks to Myerscough and McParland. These welcome four points had given the 'Villans' more than a fighting chance of avoiding relegation. With just four games left to play Villa had a six-point cushion ahead of Newcastle United and bottom-placed Sheffield Wednesday. Villa's First Division survival for another year was more or less guaranteed. In their last four matches Villa remained undefeated with two draws and two wins; most notably a 2-1 victory at Maine Road against fourth-placed Manchester City. This was Villa's fourth away win of the season, against a side that eventually finished fifth in the table. The Manchester fixture saw Nigel reach a personal landmark; he had made one-hundred first team appearances for the 'Claret and Blues.' Villa remained unbeaten in their last six games; it was their longest sequence without defeat all season. If their fortunes hadn't turned and they had continued on their losing streak they could well have rubbed shoulders with Sheffield Wednesday or Sunderland as they fell through the trap door.

Nigel felt it was time to reflect on the past few years. "I came in to the club in March '56 and I had played every game since, apart from half a dozen that I had to miss through injury. (He played in 101 games from a club total of 106 since his signing). In my first season we stayed up by the skin of our teeth while Wolves finished third. I wouldn't have swapped places for anything. I loved the club, and then to be a part of the Aston Villa team that won the Cup for the first time in nearly forty years, I just couldn't have imagined it; it's what I had dreamed of. It's just a pity we couldn't have held on to it a bit longer. It was the least the Villa supporters deserved."

Those deserving fans that Nigel referred to had voted for him to be crowned as the club's first recipient of Villa's 'Terrace Trophy.' The supporters had certainly taken this hugely committed, extremely likeable, and agile 'keeper to their hearts. Never had a goalkeeper at Aston Villa Football Club been so highly thought of since the great Sam Hardy many years before. When the season finally drew to a close, the Villa announced their forthcoming trip to Germany. As in the previous year, Villa would go on a post-season tour. They would fly to Munich on May 8th.

CHAPTER SEVEN

HOW THE MIGHTY FALL

Aston Villa's post-season tour of West Germany kicked-off less than a fortnight after the 57/58 English season concluded. Villa lost 2-1 to their first hosts, TSV 1860 Munich, but would be undefeated in the next two games, playing out draws at Aachen and Duisburg. Villa were lacking that 'killer instinct' in front of goal, both games finishing goalless.

Mediocrity was the only apt description for their previous League campaign. Four wins in the last six games had saved Villa from relegation and it was only two seasons ago they had survived only by goal average. Far too often Aston Villa were finishing the season playing for their First Division survival. The Villa shareholders wanted to get a representative into the boardroom to air their concerns.

The 58/59 campaign kicked-off on August 23rd with Villa facing bitter local rivals Birmingham City. Last season had also started with the Second City 'derby,' but with their home advantage Birmingham had taken the spoils. Aston Villa and their fans were keen to avenge that defeat, not forgetting that the 'Blues' had done the double over them for the first time in half a century. Of the eleven Villa players that kicked-off in the previous season, eight of those were in the line-up for this game. Had Jackie Sewell been fit it would have been nine. At the interval Villa were trailing in front of a crowd of 55,198. Then Stan 'the wham' Lynn rescued the home side with a successful penalty after fifty-two minutes. Villa dominated the game; Nigel wasn't called upon to make a save until ten minutes from the end of the 1-1 draw.

Two days later 'Pompey' were the visitors to the Midlands. A Billy Myerscough goal ensured the 'Villans' would go in level at half-time. After the interval and with the light fading, Villa turned on their newly-installed floodlights. Johnny Dixon was the most senior player, this being his three-hundred and ninety-eighth first team appearance in his fourteenth season with Aston Villa and he took the distinction of scoring the first 'floodlit' goal at Villa Park. It was a good night all-round and Villa went on to win the match 3-2.

The 'bright' start to the season faded badly from there: Villa suffering a run of six consecutive defeats. Conceding a whopping twenty-four goals, the Villa were at 'sixes and seven' - well almost. They were defeated 7-2 by newly-promoted West Ham United, followed by a 5-2 drubbing on the south coast at 'Pompey.'

Nigel was mortified. "It was terrible and I was being made to look like a proper chump of a 'keeper. If I hadn't been doing my job right we could have conceded double figures in every game; there was no confidence in the dressing room and rumours were rife that Eric Houghton was going to leave; yet the fans were still turning up in droves."

The rot was stopped temporarily when Villa snatched a point in a 1-1 draw at home to Blackpool. Better was to follow with back-to-back wins, a 3-2 victory at Ewood Park with Packy McParland, Gerry Hitchens and Leslie Smith doing the damage and then a 2-1 win at home to Newcastle's 'Magpies,' with the 'blooded' Ken Barrett scoring both. Barrett was on target the following week at home to West Brom, scoring his last-ever Villa goal in a 4-1 defeat.

With a dozen games gone, Villa were rooted to the foot of the First Division, with just eight points to show for their efforts. Manchester City and Everton were above them on goal average whilst Leeds had one point more.

The season had not started well and noises of discontent were emanating louder than ever from the 'inner sanctum' of Trinity Road. At the Shareholders AGM, disgruntled shareholder representatives had tried unsuccessfully to install two of their own nominees on the board, but both, retiring Directors, Bruce Normansell and Joe Broughton were re-elected.

In October, at a cost of £30,000, Eric Houghton bought in Bill Beaton from Dunfermline Athletic; he was a goalkeeper and would be available as cover for Nigel. At the time this was Aston Villa Football Club's record transfer purchase and would remain so for nearly a decade.

When the Villa made the journey up to Leeds United they could only manage a draw with their fellow strugglers, which was followed by a 2-1 defeat at home to Arsenal. Irishman Peter McParland scored but this was only his third of the campaign and Villa remained bottom, adrift by one point.

Star man McParland was so disillusioned with events at the club that he submitted a written transfer request. He had been pondering this for months; he felt he was losing confidence and form at Villa Park and that a move would be in his best interests. His request was left for the manager to open while McParland was away in Spain for a week on international duty. Some accused 'Mac' of deserting a sinking ship. Fortunately for the Midlanders, he received a vast amount of mail from supporters, the majority of which appealed for him to stay. The fans' letters had the desired effect and later on he changed his mind; and his goals would continue.

The next visitors to Villa Park were the FA Cup winners, Bolton Wanderers. They were sitting 'top of the pile' but came down from Lancashire without their talisman forward Nat Lofthouse who had been injured playing for England against Russia. Villa were first to concede, as early as the sixth minute, but before the half-time whistle blew McParland came up trumps and scored an equaliser. Just like the 'Gunners' match three days previously, the Villa lads trudged in at the break with scores level. The fans were praying the game wouldn't end the same way as the Arsenal match. Nigel kept the 'Trotters' out time and again, "I remember their wing-half being given a great chance to put the League leaders in front. It was a great cross from Neville

Bannister but Hennin headed it straight towards me, it was easier to score." Villa rode their luck and with just a minute on the watch they managed to snatch the winner from a Les Smith corner kick, Stan 'the wham' and his dapper crew-cut coming to the rescue. The bottom of the table team had toppled the League leaders. With this win under their belt the Villa moved to third from bottom and out of a relegation position; their defeat saw Bolton drop to third place.

The following Wednesday Aston Villa had a floodlit fixture against foreign opposition; it was a welcome relief to be away from the pressure of being a team at the wrong end of the League. GAIS from Gothenburg were the visitors. For all the Villa were having a torrid time of it in the domestic season, they were still streets ahead of the Swedes - they dominated the entire game and finished convincing winners at 3-0.

By November the 'Villans' were back to their losing ways. This time Kenilworth Road was the venue, where Luton remained unbeaten. For only the third time that season Villa actually held an interval lead, thanks to Gerry Hitchens knocking one in. The omens were good; on past form the Villa had claimed maximum points from the last two fixtures when they had been in that position. But Luton Town put on some intense pressure and finally it paid off. Sims and Dugdale having to stand up to the onslaught. The first Villa concession was a fierce shot from inside the area; the second was a complete freak, as Nigel explained: "The ball was hit with real venom, it caught Vic Crowe on the foot and spiralled up in the air. It sailed over me and I didn't think it was possible that the ball would drop enough to go into the net, but the bloody thing scraped the underside of the bar and in it went. You don't remember many goals that beat you, but ones like that you never forget." Everton then became the second team that season to hit Villa for four at Villa Park. Nigel brought down former Villa player Dave Hickson after just ten minutes and the

'Toffeemen' scored from the resulting penalty. But worse was yet to come. John Sharples had been understudy to Peter Aldis for the last dozen games; in this match John managed to reclaim the ball after losing possession, but was closed down unexpectedly so put the ball back to the Villa 'keeper. Nigel tried in vain, but lost this duel to Everton's inside-right Thomas, who coolly slotted the ball home. Within minutes Nigel was signalling the bench, he had torn muscles in his chest, over-stretching while trying to prevent the opposition scoring. Villa went in at the break trailing 3-0. The Villa were able to pull back two through Sewell and Hitchens in the second-half, but Everton added another goal to their three first-half strikes.

Eric Houghton took the cheque book and went out on the prowl again. This time he ventured up to the East Midlands and his old stamping ground, Meadow Lane. He returned to Villa Park with the acquired services of Glasgow born, right-half/inside-forward, Ron Wylie, who had received rave reviews on a regular basis. Next game was a short trip to Filbert Street to face Leicester City. With Nigel having to sit this one out, recent and expensive signing Bill Beaton came in to make his first team debut. Sitting at the bottom of the table, one point adrift of the Villa things looked bad for the 'Foxes' and after forty-five minutes Villa raced into a 3-1 lead with Jackie Sewell adding to Gerry Hitchens' brace. It was mid-November and for the first time all season the Villa managed to take a two-goal cushion into the second-half; but then they fell apart, conceding five goals. Leicester City who had only scored twenty-five times all season were made to look like world-beaters. The new Villa 'keeper, Beaton, had a spectacularly dreadful debut. He played his last League game that afternoon for his 'new' club, in the 6-3 defeat.

On Wednesday November 19th the Scottish League and League Cup 'double' winners, Heart of Midlothian, provided the floodlit entertainment. The luckless Beaton 'remained in the sticks' as Nigel was still nursing his chest injury. Full-back Peter Aldis returned to action after being sidelined in September at home to Forest, and Ron Wylie was the latest to be given a run out in the 'Claret and Blue' jersey. A gate of 23,000 witnessed a thrilling game of football. Vic Crowe was given the captaincy for the evening as recognition for his first Wales call-up in the forthcoming England match. Twice Villa drew level, the first one was an own goal, the second from recognised 'goal-getter', Hitchens. Now it the Scots turn to find themselves chasing the game, after Peter 'Mac' put the hosts a goal up. Unfortunately the lead was held for no more than a dozen minutes. This was a great advert for the game; both sides played good, fast-flowing football that was greatly appreciated by the paying public. The match ended all-square, 3-3. Eric Houghton made his way to the dressing room after the match. With tears in his eyes, he told his players that he had resigned.

Immediately after this friendly, Aston Villa Football Club issued an official statement that their manager, Mr Eric Houghton, had left the club by 'mutual consent.' Which, when you cut to the chase, meant that Eric had been given the choice of 'jump or be pushed.' During the last week of November' amidst all of the changes and turmoil, Alan Deakin signed for the Villa as a professional.

Two more games remained in November. Preston North End were seen off at Villa Park, 2-0, and then at Turf Moor a solitary Hitchens' goal was insufficient as Burnley finished the game 3-1 winners.

At the start of December there was no manager at Villa Park. A 1-1 draw at home to Manchester City's 'Blues' was followed by Villa's second away win of the campaign, this time in North London, at League leaders Arsenal. Myerscough and McParland bagged the goals that would see the Villa knock the current League leaders off the top for the second time this season. Unlike the Bolton victory, it didn't haul Villa from the foot of the table. Just when they thought things couldn't get any worse, their bitter rivals from the Small Heath District of 'Brum' put four past them for the first time in their history. Things were looking bleak.

On Christmas Eve and four days after the St Andrews debacle, Aston Villa appointed their new manager. The boardroom opted for Sheffield United manager, Joe Mercer, though he wasn't the choice of a few first team stars. Les Smith, Nigel Sims and Jackie Sewell all feared the worst, expecting Mercer would want 'out with the old and in with the new' talent. Joe signed his five-year contract with Aston Villa then hot-footed it back to the north to watch Sheffield United, the team he had just left, play at Grimsby Town on Christmas Day. After that match, he went over to Manchester to watch 'his' new side play Matt Busby's Manchester United. Villa lost 2-1 after being all level at the break. Had games finished at the interval, Villa would have accumulated another nine points by the end of the campaign. A crowd of 56,450 packed into Villa Park to see the traditional festive return match when Manchester United took both points, denying the Villa the opportunity to score in the game.

For Nigel, and others at the club, it looked like there were some uncertain times ahead, "I think Eric went late November or early December 1958, but either way I remember there was at least a few weeks where we had no manager and we all wondered what was going to happen. Barely a week after Joe Mercer had been appointed the new manager, Leslie Smith had come to me and said he could just sense he was going to be shown the door at Villa Park. Leslie had been a favourite of Wolverhampton Wanderers manager Stan Cullis before the Villa, and that sometimes rubbed a new boss up the wrong way, but Joe also liked a younger team brought through the ranks and that wasn't us." It seemed there was 'no smoke without fire' and Mercer's early evaluation of his new club had started something smouldering. His conclusion was that the place was morbid and lifeless. He said it seemed like the club was being choked by tradition - a wonderful friend but a dangerous enemy.

Aston Villa started the New Year of 1958, in much the same manner as they saw out the last, by losing yet another home game the following weekend against West Ham United, who were placed comfortably in mid-table. They had taken maximum points from the Villa, who were firmly planted in the basement. In the process of beating them 2-1, the 'Hammers' had penetrated the Villa's defences nine times during both games. When Monday came, Dick Taylor, Mercer's right-hand man, took up the newly-created post of Assistant Manager.

Nigel remembers the state of play shortly after Mercer moved in. "He came in and we lost our first three games. He knew he had to act fast, so he started getting the players to 'double-up' on opponents. If we lost possession we had to do all we could to regain it. The outfield players were covering miles on the training pitch, playing to the style Mercer wanted. A lot of clubs play like that nowadays, but back then it was all new, we were pioneers if you like."

A welcome break from the misery of a First Division fight for survival came in the form of an FA Cup tie. As the weeks went on it was looking more likely that their efforts were just failing in the League. The tie gave the fans and the players something to look forward to. A good crowd of 33,923 braved the bitter weather and turned out for the second weekend of the New Year. Even the most pessimistic of supporters expected the 'Villans' to be too much for struggling Second Division outfit Rotherham United. The omens looked good, Villa had faced the 'Merry Millers' once before in a Cup tie and had won 3-1 back in 52/53. But the South Yorkshire side started in a fashion that wasn't in keeping with their lowly League position. A shot narrowly flashed by an upright and then Nigel was called upon to charge down a shot from a hesitating Webster. It took until the second-half for the Villa to get their noses in front through Sewell. Then a headed goal eighteen minutes from time by Rotherham forward Sawyer had the large Yorkshire contingent yelling with excitement, dreaming of a bumper pay day taking the mighty Midlanders back up to Millmoor. Their dreams were shattered five minutes later when Villa's Jackie Sewell cleverly brought the ball down for Hitchens to stroke home. Due to some terrible weather the distraction from League football continued with the Villa's trip to Nottingham Forest postponed; the fourth-round Cup tie was played before the resumption of League matches. This tie was no pushover, offering far tougher opposition in the shape of Chelsea, who had home advantage and former Villa wing-half Stan Crowther. Jimmy Greaves had Chelsea one-up after five minutes, when Dugdale, attempting a pass back to Nigel, stumbled, "When you made a mistake like that in front of the League's leading scorer there was only one thing he was going to do with it and that was 'stick it away." The Villa didn't hang their heads though and with every passing minute they improved and the confidence that had built up in the defence spread to the forward line. Through Hitchens and Myerscough Villa went into a 2-1 lead and had the upper hand at the break. Chelsea's attackers were kept to trying long-range shots that hardly troubled Nigel, who was a confident 'keeper. They just couldn't find the net again and at the finish it was Aston Villa who went into the hat for the fifth-round draw.

When the weather improved the League fixtures resumed, with Villa welcoming Chelsea to Villa Park and winning 3-1. The much-needed two points were not sufficient to lift Villa from the foot of the table but it did put them on level pegging with 'Pompey.' Villa had conceded more goals than everyone, bar

Portsmouth, but had the distinction of worst goal average. It had taken a month and a day, but Manager Mercer had tasted his first League victory as boss.

Villa took a win in February, sandwiched between two defeats. The Cup had thrown up a difficult tie at Goodison Park, but Villa brought Everton's run to an end, with a convincing 4-1 victory. Ron Wylie was on the score sheet for the first time, and the second and third! The icing on the cake came when Peter 'Mac' added one to Wylie's hat-trick. The 'Toffees' had reached the fifth round the easy way, by defeating two second flight sides, Sunderland and Charlton. Villa new boy Doug 'Jock' Winton a Scottish 'B' international, signed from Burnley two weeks before, was blooded in the fifth-round tie.

On February 28th, in front of 60,145, their biggest crowd of the season, Villa met Burnley to decide who would go through to the semi-finals. Luckily it had been a home draw, as Villa had always struggled at Turf Moor. But contrary to the expectations of the huge gate, the hosts weren't able to raise their game as they had in previous away rounds. The most notable incident of the 0-0 lacklustre draw was, as Nigel remembers. "The referee had to be carried off, a linesman came on in his place and after a loud-speaker announcement a gentleman appeared from the packed terraces to run the line. He was running up and down in his trousers and blazer; he didn't help us though and we ended up going to Burnley's place. We thought we had blown it."

Off to Lancashire for the inevitable. Villa hadn't tasted success in Burnley's back yard since September 1936, when they had been in the Second Division for the only time in their eighty-five-year history. Nigel managed to look on the optimistic side. "Well, we had given our fans something to cheer about, and the confidence gathered from those Cup ties had pushed us to safety in the League, so it hadn't all been bad."

The replay was on the following Tuesday, with Villa making

one change from the first leg. Leslie Smith replaced Myerscough. The Villa side:

> Sims, Aldis, Winton, Dixon, Dugdale, Crowe, Smith, Sewell, Hitchens, Wylie, McParland.

Peter McParland did the damage at Turf Moor with two finely executed second-half goals. Nigel set up the second, "I sent a long ball up to Ron (Wylie) who passed the ball over to Peter (McParland) who was on the half way line. He turned his man and ran, kept on running, and put the ball past the Burnley 'keeper Colin McDonald, who was coming out to meet him - that was a great individual goal." That day victory belonged to the Midlands outfit, 2-0, at the final whistle. The Burnley fans really didn't like the Irishman facing their side, he was becoming a nemesis to them in the Cup. It was his goal, two seasons ago in the quarter-finals at Burnley that had given the Villa another crack at the 'Clarets,' and when the Villa Park replay came he even bagged the second of the night. Just two seasons after winning the trophy, Aston Villa Football Club were back in the semi-finals for a record sixteenth appearance.

Villa played twice as many League fixtures in March than they had in February. The month started well, in fact far better than any dared to hope. Leeds went home pointless after a 2-1 defeat with Sewell and Hitchens netting. This win actually lifted Villa out of the relegation spot, putting them one point ahead of Leicester and two above 'Pompey.' McParland had his work cut out though if he was to retain his title of leading scorer. Nigel recalled, "Gerry was giving it a real go, he was like Jimmy Greaves, if there was a chance going then he was in the thick of it. We were conceding too many goals at the back, but if they, Peter and Gerry, were on form we knew we stood a chance."

With a win under their belts from their last League match, Villa travelled up to Sheffield from Buxton on the morning of the semi-final with great confidence. A crowd of 64,882 at Hillsborough greeted the Aston Villa and Nottingham Forest teams on to the pitch. The game settled into a midfield contest, with the 'keepers of both clubs being called upon very little. Thomson, in the Forest goal, was the first to make real saves. He kept McParland out, as well as Dixon moments later. It was 0-0 at half-time, and Villa were still expected to reach the final. After the break, Forest came out more determined, and in a match that never quite reached the heights, it was Quigley, their young inside-right who managed to convert a cross and take the East Midlands side onto Wembley Empire Stadium. Aston Villa's Cup run had ended; survival in the League was now the order of the day. Nigel remembered the mixed emotions of that afternoon. "Gerry Hitchens blamed himself for the semi-final defeat. He had this lucky old coin and he carried it with him everywhere. Well, before the Forest game, Gerry was getting in a panic, he'd mislaid his lucky charm. We went out of the Cup and then the following week, when it (the coin) turned back up, he started scoring again! He scored the week before the Cup game and straight after the Forest match he scored three in one week and two in the next! It's not sour grapes, but we should have had a draw at least on the day. Packy had the ball in the net and the ref gave it as offside. When it was pointed out to him that their defender was on the line, he said that Packy had handled the ball that incidentally was on the floor, so that wasn't right. The lads were all adamant that the Forest full-back Whare had handled the ball while he was laid down in the area and that it was impossible for the ref not to have seen it. We left Hillsborough feeling a bit cheated."

The next game was a toughie. Bolton were smarting after Villa had knocked them off top place back in October. Now they were in fourth and had won twelve of their home games. Burnden Park was a bit of a fortress. Gerry hadn't read the script, as his hat-trick in a 3-1 win convinced football watchers that Aston Villa were going to do their usual 'Houdini act' and sidestep the First Division trap door.

Hitchens was on target again in the next match, twice! That was six goals in three games for the forward. Luton came up to Villa Park only three points and three places higher than Villa, but lost 3-1 with a Leslie Smith penalty rounding off the scoreline.

Nine games left, the Villa had left it late, but they had started to climb, now it was a question of how high? They had a five-point cushion over the bottom two teams and the next three teams, all on twenty-seven points above them, could be overtaken with one more win.

Peter McParland was trailing his strike partner Hitchens by five goals. 'Mac' had bagged twelve to Gerry's seventeen, prior to Villa's visit to Tottenham. 'Spurs' were also having a hard time compared to last season's highflying campaign, when they had finished in third position. Compared with the Villa, they were two places higher and three points better-off with twenty-nine on the board, against Villa's twenty-six, though Villa had a game in hand. That day 'Spurs' ran out 3-2 winners with Mac hitting a double. 'Packy' found the net the following day, away at Everton, where the Villa players thought they had been robbed of at least a point by the referee. Former Villa player Hickson pushed Jimmy Dugdale to the ground from behind. The Villa centre-half stood up and expected to see the ref award him a free kick, instead he pointed for a penalty to Everton! On the following Monday, 'Spurs' visit to Villa Park brought a welcome point, with 'Packy' adding another goal to his tally - he had hit a rich vein of form; Villa needed it more now, than ever before. Their safety cushion was down to two points, they had to stop their slide and reverse it fast!

They moved into the final month knowing there were just six games left to save their top-flight status. Leicester City, who were two points adrift of the Villa, came to Villa Park and gave their own survival chances a huge boost by taking both points in a game totally dominated by the home side, who just couldn't convert any of their numerous chances. By now Portsmouth were as good as down, being six points adrift of safety. Villa were in a safer place, with Leicester behind on goal average. But the following weekend, former Aston Villa player, Tommy Thompson, showed no mercy for his ex-teammates when he hit a double as Preston North End beat them 4-2. Villa threw away their advantage after the interval, having led 2-1 through Sewell and Myerscough. Desperately running out of games and ideas Villa had one last home game before finishing the campaign followed by three away games. Burnley left Villa Park, satisfied they had restricted 'Packy's' goal attempts and, with the whistle blowing at 0-0, had earned a point. On the same afternoon, the 'Foxes' of Leicester went to near rivals Nottingham Forest and playing them off the park winning 4-1, had done themselves a huge favour. Their win meant they leap-frogged Manchester City, who seemed to have taken a leaf out of the Villa's book and gone into freefall. In mid-March Manchester City had been sitting in eighteenth place, not good, but certainly safe and out of harm's way. Then they went on a run of nine games without a win picking up only two points out of a possible eighteen. Their penultimate match of the campaign was a 0-0 draw at home to Villa. Villa had gone to Forest between the Burnley and Man City matches, but whereas Forest had lost their last home game to Leicester City 4-1, they turned that result on its head and sent Villa packing with nothing, having defeated them 2-0. To make matters worse, Leslie Smith played for the last time in a 'Claret and Blue' jersey. Villa were without a game plan and it was obvious the team had no confidence running through it. The season had nearly run its course. The relegation decider had gone right 'to the wire.' Portsmouth had known their fate for a long time, they had finished their season that weekend with twenty-one points, eight adrift of Villa and Man City. Now it was a case of simple maths.

To finish the season were a deciding Midland 'derby' between West Bromwich Albion and Aston Villa' and in the north-west, Manchester City playing Leicester City. A Villa win would see them safe; a Manchester City loss would also see the Villa safe. What happened was that Leicester, who had been assured of safety, went down 3-1, not the result Aston Villa wanted. Then the Albion would do their rivals no favours - even if they had been bribed! It was 0-0 at the Hawthorns at half-time and at this point Joe Mercer decided to go to attend a banquet at Wolverhampton celebrating Billy Wright's one-hundredth cap. He would be unaware of the fate of 'his' team. The result of this game couldn't be underestimated; it would be arguably the biggest match in Villa's recent history. Hitchens scored for Villa, their first goal in four games. Villa had the vital goal, though there were still twenty-two minutes of play left. "The clock seemed like it had stopped," said Nigel, "Albion pushed everything they could at us and the ref kept looking at his watch. I pulled off two saves and with minutes remaining they got the equaliser that we were so desperate to keep out. We went up field in vain. Their defenders were kicking the ball into the stands to run the clock down and then - the final whistle went; you'd have thought the 'Baggies' had won the bloody League! We stood in the rain trying to make sense of it. Our captain hung his head in total misery; Pat Saward dropped to his knees in the mud, and where was our manager eh? He wasn't bloody there! He found out the result later that evening."

This was only the second time in Aston Villa Football Club's history that they would be playing in the Second Division.

Leslie Smith's concerns back in the December, when Mercer was appointed, never came to anything as he continued to play his normal orthodox position as outside-right for Aston Villa; but only until the end of that season, when an Achilles tendon injury forced him out of the game. He never did find out if he was Mercer's type of player or not.

CHAPTER EIGHT

GUNNER SIMS

The 58/59 season had finally drawn to a close on April 29th at the Hawthorns. A draw there wasn't enough to stop Aston Villa being relegated for only the second time in their history. Nigel didn't have time to dwell on what had been a difficult season or think about the next one, where he would be plying his trade in the second flight for the first time in his career. Any reflections would have to be put to the back of his mind. Joe Mercer called him into his office and put a proposition to him. Mercer wanted a favour from Nigel although from his tone; it wasn't so much of being asked, as being told what was happening. It was also pointed out to him it wouldn't do his career any harm if he went along with it.

George Swindin had been appointed manager of Arsenal the previous year, after impressing as the boss of Peterborough United. He had amassed a total of two-hundred and seventy-two appearances for the Gunners as their first-choice 'keeper back in the 1950s and had been a former teammate of Joe Mercer's. The two played together when Arsenal had won the 1950 FA Cup Final, with Mercer as Captain and being first to hold aloft the trophy.

Swindin and Mercer went back a long way remaining friends as their careers had taken different directions; but now they both managed two of the biggest football teams in English football.

In the season that had just ended, Arsenal had finished third in the table, but had been very unfortunate to lose their regular goalkeeper, Welsh international Jack Kelsey, through injury. He had missed the last three months of the season after breaking his arm in a 0-0 draw with Manchester City at Maine Road. Their stand-in 'keeper, Jim Standen was drafted in for the remainder of the campaign, but suffered a strained back. Peter Goy was third choice; he made two first team appearances for the Gunners and played Arsenal's final game of the season at home,

118

to Birmingham City on May 4th.

Arsenal had commitments to do a post-season tour and were due to fly to Italy and then Switzerland where they would play three prestigious friendlies; the first game due to be played ten days after the Birmingham match. Their top 'keeper was still months away from being fit; to make matters worse Kelsey's replacement was also crocked, and third choice Goy was unable to travel as he was on National Service.

Swindin, having been a 'keeper himself, could appreciate what an immense talent Aston Villa had in Nigel Sims. The fact that his old friend Mercer was Sims' Manager might hold the answer to his predicament, but there was only one way to find out. Swindin made the call to Mercer - could Nigel Sims guest for Arsenal FC on their tour?

Arsenal had already made enquiries with the relevant governing bodies regarding their dilemma. Due to their heavy injury list both the Football Association and the Football League sanctioned the loan deal.

Nigel didn't particularly like being backed into a corner, but it would not have helped his career much if he had chosen to snub the Manager. With that in mind he decided to go, "I would rather have stayed home, I had things I needed to do which you can only sort out in the close season, but I didn't really have a choice in it. Certainly not with having a £30,000 'keeper, Beaton, waiting in the wings. Besides, playing football didn't feel a job to me. It was a sheer pleasure, and going to play in a lovely setting like Italy, testing yourself against some of the greatest players in the world would have done me more good than sitting at home, pondering what life in Division Two would have in store for me."

Nigel didn't have time on his side; the North London 'Gunners' were flying out on Tuesday May 12th. He hurried with making arrangements, then travelled down to the capital, where he was quickly introduced to his new temporary manager, teammates and more importantly, the defenders with whom he would be working closely.

The team flew off to Italy and after a few very brief training sessions, Nigel took his place in the Arsenal line-up to face the Italian giants Juventus, on their home patch in Turin. Included in their line-up was 'Il Gigante Buono' - the gentle giant, John Charles. John had left Britain and Leeds United just the August before, to play in Serie A for 'Juve,' after the Italians had watched him smash one-hundred and fifty goals in fewer than three-hundred appearances for the Yorkshire side. "Playing against 'Big John' was an experience, he was phenomenal in the air, as good as it got! He 'took no prisoners' and you certainly knew you had been in a game, but he was fair and he was a true gentleman. I don't think he ever got cautioned in his entire career, a smashing bloke."

Arsenal lost 3-1 to Juventus, their lone scorer being none other than 'Big John's' younger brother, Mel Charles, the 'Gunners' centre-half/centre-forward. "Juventus had another forward that night, Omar Sivori, he caused us a load of grief. Omar was tiny but what a terror! He was great with his left foot, very good with his right and even good with his head. Tommy Docherty said he would sort him out but he couldn't, and neither could Dave Bowen. No one kept the five-feet four-inch Argentinean quiet - John Charles and Omar Sivori, 'little and large,' what a pair!"

The next game took place six days later, on May 20th, when Arsenal faced Fiorentina. The 'Gunners' won 2-1 on the night with their goals coming from Jackie Henderson and Jimmy Bloomfield. Nigel picked up an injury in this game, which meant he would sit out the last match to be played in Switzerland.

The Arsenal party left Italy and flew to southern Switzerland and the city of Lugano, "It was a beautiful place, nestled right on the banks of Lake Lugano known as the 'Monaco of Switzerland.' You drew back the curtains in the hotel room and saw this lake with the mountains in the background. It was incredible; the view would take your breath away." In football terms, FC Lugano were not opposition of the calibre of Juve or Fiorentina, but Arsenal were a big crowd-puller, so a 'good gate' was expected at the little Cornaredo Stadium that had been built in 1951. "The ground wasn't big like Villa Park or Molineux, but it was a nice compact little place and the Swiss gave it a real go when the whistle went." Nigel was a spectator and watched Jim Standen take his place 'between the sticks' and concede just the one goal. His teammates did their jobs adequately enough and Arsenal wound up their post-season tour with a resounding 4-1 victory. The 'Gunners' scorers were Henderson, Bloomfield, Charles and the fourth was an own goal.

Although Nigel had only played two matches for Arsenal, their Board had been sufficiently impressed by what they had seen and what George Swindin had told them. On Arsenal's return to England an offer of £60,000 was submitted to Aston Villa for the services of Nigel Sims. They knew that Kelsey was still a long way from returning to first team action. But Nigel was going nowhere - apart from little outposts such as Scunthorpe United, Lincoln City, Bristol Rovers and Leyton Orient, all in Division Two - and he would be going alongside his 'Claret and Blue' teammates.

Kelsey was missing from the 'Gunners' side until October 24th, and as Nigel remained at the Villa, Arsenal were faced with relying on the talents of Jim Standen or looking elsewhere.

CHAPTER NINE

IN A DIFFERENT LEAGUE

Alex Massie and Eric Houghton, both players and managers alike for the Villa, Fred Biddlestone and full-backs Ernie 'Mush' Callaghan and George Cummings. Bob Iverson, Freddie Haycock, Frankie Broome and Ronnie Starling - all Aston Villa legends and men remembered fondly in conversations by generations throughout Aston Villa households. These were the men who dragged the famous Midlands club back to where they rightfully belonged - Division One.

The latest generation of fans had been brought up watching Aston Villa dining exclusively from 'the top table' - until now. They would taste life 'on the other side' this coming campaign.

Sims, Lynn, Dugdale, Saward and McParland were Villa heroes and the men who had brought Cup victory back to Aston for the first time since Andy Ducat had lifted the FA Cup in 1920. They formed the backbone of the side, assisted by a new breed of players, Crowe, Hitchens, and Wylie. Recent Mercer signings that season were inside-forward Bobby Thomson from Wolves; Jimmy MacEwan, an outside-right from Raith Rovers, Jimmy Adam outside-left from Luton; and John Neal, a full-back from Swindon. Add a pinch of 'Mercer's Minors' - Deakin, Burrows and Tindall and the result - a band of would-be heroes who held the future fortunes of Aston Villa Football Club. They were all there to do a job and they would have to step up to the mark.

Billy Myerscough, Peter Aldis and Leslie Smith were all '57 Cup winners, but played no further part in the 'Claret and Blues' future; they didn't feature again in the first team before being shipped out to other clubs. Smith had predicted that his days were numbered after Houghton's replacement had been unveiled. Nigel might have made it four, had the Villa board decided to accept the £60,000 Arsenal had put on the table after his heroics in Italy against 'Juve.' Joe Mercer was not going to stand in his way. Other departures were lesser-known players, many who had never appeared for the first team including a certain Ron Atkinson!

Climbing out of Division Two was going to be a challenging task. For smaller teams, such as Rotherham, Lincoln, Leyton Orient, Bristol Rovers, Brighton & Hove Albion and Scunthorpe United, teams who had never scaled Division One heights, Aston Villa's visit would guarantee big crowds, record gate receipts, and in some cases record attendances. For the 'Villans' every week would be like a Cup Final. "The smaller, less fashionable sides were desperate to keep us down there with them. Their supporters would turn out in droves and so would ours. It was a chance for Villa fans to get to new, smaller outposts. You have to remember the Villa were still regarded as a 'big fish' and they, the minor teams didn't want us escaping," remarked Nigel, whose job it was to keep those Second Division hotshots at bay.

As Villa looked towards the future, they took on two young Scottish full-backs, Charlie Aitken and Wilson Briggs, although the job at hand was not forgotten, or underestimated. Pat Saward was made captain for the forthcoming campaign. Nigel remembers an inspiring pep talk: "Joe Mercer, Dick Taylor and Ray Shaw sat down with us all after one training session. They told us that we, Aston Villa, would rise to the heights again, maybe not this season, just that we would. We were conditioned for First Division football and the longer we were down in the Second Division, the harder it would be to get out. The teams that were expected to be up there challenging us would be Sheffield United, Liverpool and possibly Cardiff City. These were sides we needed to take maximum points off."

Brighton & Hove Albion had first crack at the 'fallen giants' from 'Brum.' Villa blooded three players at the Goldstone Ground; Jimmy Adam, Jimmy MacEwan and youngster Terry Morrell at left-half. Morrell impressed that afternoon, clearing-off the line twice. McEwan scored his first goal in 'Claret and Blue' that afternoon and Sewell, his predecessor, scored his last. Villa had started their season satisfactorily, a 2-1 win, both points in the bag. Then four days later came a match at Roker Park, and Villa were beaten 1-0. Playing in this game Nigel chalked up his one-hundred and fiftieth first team appearance for the 'Claret and Blues.' He couldn't have wished for anything more since moving from the 'Old Gold outfit.' "It came around so quick, one-hundred and fifty games is quite a landmark; you know it only took me three seasons at Villa to rack them up; I was at Molineux for nearly three times longer and played only a quarter of the games I managed with the Villa."

In a reversal of fortunes, the Villa inside-right, Jackie Sewell, made his last-ever appearance in a Villa jersey that day. Jackie, like Les Smith, had known the 'writing was on the wall,' it was a question of 'when, not if.' During his time at Notts County and Sheffield Wednesday, Jackie was in his own words, "a cheeky young whippersnapper," who took delight in giving left-backs and centre-halves such as Mercer, who was playing for Arsenal, 'a bit of a chasing.' "We never got pally with our direct opponents, right-wingers against left-backs and the like, it never happened; yes, I was a cheeky 'young un,' never thought much about where it might lead."

Villa followed their defeat at Sunderland with two successive home games; Swansea, then Sunderland, when Villa would be hoping to gain revenge against the 'Rokermen.'

Nigel was a bit surprised at the time, "I thought coming down a Division would be a bit easier, but if it was anything like what Len Allchurch served up, it was going to be a long, hard season. I remember Len's brother, Ivor, was supposed to be the bigger name, but that day, on the right-wing for Swansea, Allchurch was fantastic. He kept me busy all afternoon. Luckily, his crosses weren't converted and through Peter McParland we got a 1-0 win and both points." A Hitchens' brace and Bobby

Thomson scoring his first Villa goal, saw them exact revenge on Sunderland, only five days after their Roker Park encounter, with a comfortable 3-0 win. However, the next fixture saw Aston Villa sailing into uncharted waters at Eastville Stadium, home of Bristol Rovers. They had never played the 'Pirates' before and didn't know what to expect, but settled for a 1-1 draw; although it should have been both points and not a share. "We had shots cleared off their line and the Rovers' goalie Norman got down to save a few times when it looked certain we would score - at least from where I was standing at the other end," commented Nigel.

After a steady start, Aston Villa were second in the table, just on the shoulder of Sheffield United. With six more fixtures remaining in the month of September, Villa went on a goal scoring spree, bagging fifteen goals, amassing eleven out of a possible twelve points. Their good home form continued, with victories against Ipswich, 3-1, and Portsmouth, 5-2.

When they played away to Huddersfield Town, it proved to be no obstacle, and the points were gratefully accepted by the Villa, through a 'Packy" solitary goal. Defeating Leyton Orient 1-0 at Villa Park in front of a 40,860 crowd maintained their one-hundred per cent home record equalling the promising start they had achieved back in the 53/54 season.

In the first ten fixtures of the new campaign Nigel conceded only seven goals, keeping four clean sheets. The strikers did their job with equal efficiently and put away nineteen at the other end. If they continued with this form, Villa had a good chance of climbing out of Division Two at the first attempt. They closed the month with a difficult trip to Stoke City. Luckily, they had suffered no injuries and Villa's line-up remained unchanged for the eighth game in a row:

Sims, Lynn, Neal, Crowe, Dugdale, Saward, MacEwan, Thomson, Hitchens, Wylie, McParland.

Villa came away with a single point after a very entertaining 3-3 draw: Stoke raced into a two-goal lead, netting both in a six-minute spell. Villa halved the deficit through a Stoke own goal, which should have been credited to the Villa outside-left, McParland. He was acknowledged as scoring the other two goals, though, to put the men from Aston 3-2 up and in the driving seat. If the forwards hadn't squandered chances galore, Stoke wouldn't have been able to level the game and secure the point they'd hardly deserved. These latest strikes took the Irishman's tally to eight for the season - not bad at all for only eleven games. Nigel was disappointed with a draw at the Victoria Ground. "After our previous five wins on the run, it felt almost like a defeat. We were really unlucky to find ourselves two-down, but we still knew we were due something from the game and should have had all three points. But that's the way it goes."

Aston Villa were now sitting proudly at the top of the Division with a three-point cushion over Cardiff City, and four points ahead of Charlton Athletic. Tides of fortune appeared to be turning since, signing terms that season, Bobby Thomson had weighed in with a few cracking goals. Now McParland and Hitchens didn't have the monopoly on 'Claret and Blue' goals, but they did have more support from other goal poachers, and the tightest defence in the Division. For the following game, Peter 'Mac' returned to Belfast on international duty and Jimmy Adam stood in for him. Again, the boys from 'Brum' found themselves in an unfamiliar outpost at Sincil Bank. Bottom of the table Lincoln City squeezed 13,812 folks into their tiny ground, a record attendance at the time. The 'Imps' had lost eight of their ten matches, but managed to square up to and earn a draw against the League leaders. They were fortunate enough to meet an off-form Villa side that afternoon and in fact were desperately unlucky not to have beaten them.

During the week, Bob Brocklebank, the former Birmingham City manager, popped into Villa Park. Standing on the terrace and having a cigarette, Bob stood chatting with the Villa boss, whilst watching the Villa lads training alongside the pitch. When Joe Mercer walked away, Brocklebank, who was now manager of fellow Second Division side Hull City, struck up a conversation with Jackie Sewell, which continued in the café on Witton Lane. When Jackie returned he went straight to the Villa's secretary office, to tell Fred Archer he was leaving to join Hull City. On October 8th 1959 Jackie Sewell ended his Villa career and another '57 Cup winner was gone.

For the coming month, Villa announced floodlit friendlies against Rapid Vienna and Raith Rovers; the latter's visit was part of the package that had brought Jackie Sewell's replacement, Jimmy MacEwan, down from north of the Border.

The next League match was against Sheffield United at Bramall Lane, where United had set the pace early on in the title race. Nigel had good reason to remember this game. "We had been in the lead for a minute or so when I got caught in the face, I had to go off, blood was everywhere and I had to have stitches, three or four I think. While I was in the dressing room I could hear the noise from the crowd on the terracing above us - they had scored or got a penalty. When I came back it turned out that 'Doc' Pace, who used to play for us, had scored for Sheffield. He was a good mate of mine, 'Doc'." The game finished 1-1.

On October 17th, a healthy crowd of 35,362 turned out to watch Villa beat Middlesbrough, thanks to full-back Stan Lynn's goal. 'Boro' had come down from Teeside, sitting third in the table, having lost only one game more than their opponents.

From their next two matches, Villa took three points. When they won at home against Plymouth Argyle they had stretched their one-hundred per cent home record to seven games. It was the Villa Park of old, becoming a fortress once again.

The month of November started with a hiccup when Villa lost their first game of the season at Anfield, 2-1. Pat Saward's old lodger Dave Hickson, hit both goals - one more than he managed in a dozen games for Villa. Now people would see if the Blues' had the mettle to bounce back.

Charlton Athletic were next at Villa Park and Hitchens, who hadn't found the back of the net in his last four games, was called into Mercer's office on the morning of the game and told he was going to be dropped. McParland had scored four goals during Gerry's drought and, being a forward who was still delivering, his position was safe. However, Hitchens pleaded his case, and won a reprieve. It was a damp and dismal day; perhaps that explained the attendance figure of 21,921, Villa's lowest crowd of the season, by quite a margin. But the hardy bunch was rewarded for braving such conditions watching as Villa tore Charlton Athletic to shreds. By the interval, Villa had raced into an unassailable lead of 4-1. It had taken Hitchens one-hundred and twenty seconds to find the net! Credit to Charlton, they didn't hang their heads and tried to make a game of it. After twenty minutes, they levelled the score. Then Thomson put Villa 2-1 up, before Hitchens was involved grabbing two more goals before the break and another two in the space of three minutes into the second-half. Outstanding! The 'Latics" goalie, Willie Duff, dislocated his finger trying to stop goal number six. Their left-back took up position between the posts but after he'd picked the ball out of the net three times, he decided it was someone else's turn! With Villa Park shouting for ten, the lads duly obliged; then added one more for good measure. Final score, 11-1!

Villa remained at the top by one point, with Cardiff City hanging on as best they could. Villa then took two more victories; the first, at Bristol City, followed by a home win against Scunthorpe United. This was the 'Irons' first, and also their last ever visit, to Villa Park for a League fixture. Both the Bristol and the Scunthorpe games finished 5-0; the Villa had notched twenty-one goals in three matches and of these Hitchens had helped himself to ten and 'Mac' had poked in five.

Villa's next game was at second placed Rotherham United, who were three points behind them. Villa had scored more goals than any other side in the Division and boasted the meanest defence. Millmoor was packed, another record attendance with Villa visiting. The home crowd watched as their side managed to do what only two other teams had managed that season - they sent Aston Villa back to the Midlands pointless. Jimmy Adam scored Villa's only goal in the 2-1 defeat, his first for the club, and Alan Deakin made his debut for the 'Brummies,' in what would turn out to be a long and eventful 'Claret and Blue' career. Nigel knew Villa had to pick themselves up as they had the last time they were beaten. "The first thing we wanted to do when we came off a pitch having lost, was to go straight back out and set the record straight. We had come back both times after losing to go on a winning spree, and that's the mark of fighters." And so it proved again. Villa took three straight victories, scoring six goals and letting in just one. With the exception of Adam scoring, McParland and Hitchens netted the remainder. They were almost neck and neck, Hitchens trailing by one goal, eightenn-nineteen. Villa then played at Hull City's Boothferry Park on Boxing Day and took both points, with Hull City making the return visit to Villa Park, forty-eight hours later. This was their first visit to the Midlanders' famous old ground. Their defenders acquitted themselves admirably in front of their fans taking a much needed point in a 1-1 draw which kept them within touching distance of nineteenth placed Bristol City. Villa had so much of the possession in their opponents half, it left 'keeper Nigel virtually unemployed and he spent most of the game jumping up and down and doing various other exercises, in order to keep warm!

This was the first point dropped at Villa Park, after eleven straight wins, which had created a new club record, breaking the previous run of ten wins, set in the League's inaugural year of 1888/89 when Villa lost their last home game of the season to the eventual Champions, Preston North End. The Hull match saw another 'Mercer Minor,' Mike Tindall, 'the latest off the conveyor belt' make his first team debut. He came in at inside-right and although during the game he was brought down in the area, nothing came of it.

The New Year saw Villa cross the Welsh border for a trip to Swansea Town's Vetch Field. Bobby Thomson scored a double and Gerry Hitchens took the other in a 3-1 win. Norman Ashe made his debut becoming the Club's youngest ever League player. 'Tosh' was the tender age of sixteen-years and forty-eight-days.

The FA Cup draw had been kind to the Villa, giving what they had wished for - a home tie. Leeds United were to be their opponents, and, although they were a top-flight team, they were struggling. Villa, having won eleven, drawn one and remaining undefeated in their home League fixtures, felt the Cup tie held no fear for them. Aston Villa had progressed to the final four in the previous year's competition, quite a feat in a season where their other performances left a lot to be desired. As they rode the crest of their Second Division wave, over 43,000 spectators watched them come from a goal down. Yet again Peter McParland had his name on the score sheet. Also Ron Wylie's cross curled in and off the post to give the bemused Scot his fifth strike of the season, the Villa's 2-1 victory ensured passage to the next round. When the draw was made, Villa's ball was last in the bag along with one other but it was Chelsea's that came out first. It was to be a repeat of last season's fourth round.

With the FA Cup Third Round safely negotiated, it was time to get back to First Division football. There were two League games to play before the Stamford Bridge Cup tie so first they tackled Bristol Rovers at home. Vic Crowe made the headlines, scoring his first goal in five years, Jimmy Adam netted one and Bobby Thomson hit his second brace in as many games. Villa cruised on to a convincing 4-1 victory. The following weekend, the 'Villans' tasted their fourth defeat of the campaign, in Suffolk, when they lost 2-1 to Alf Ramsay's Ipswich Town. The game had reached the eightieth minute scoreless and had a draw written all over it. Then, Villa centre-half Dugdale attempted to clear a cross, but watched with dismay as his header was diverted beyond the reach of Nigel into his own net. Five minutes later, Jimmy was on the score sheet again, but this time at the right end and Villa were all-square. With time nearly up Nigel beat out a shot and the ball fell kindly to Town striker Crawford who connected sweetly - bang, it was in the back of the net! 'Nigger' was in real England form that day and at times he stood alone between Ipswich and a certain goal. One point-blank save from Owen earned him a rapturous ovation from the crowd. In spite of this defeat, Villa remained two points clear at the top, just ahead of a very determined Cardiff City, who had a four-point cushion over third-placed Rotherham United.

When the Stamford Bridge Cup tie came around, it wasn't just Villa that had suffered recent defeats. Chelsea had also taken 'knock backs;' one such loss, was at home to a Leeds United side that had shipped more goals than any other side in the top two Divisions, with the exception of Plymouth Argyle. Stamford Bridge's highest attendance of the season was set that afternoon, when a crowd of 66,671 turned out to see if Chelsea could progress a stage further than they had the year before. Fortune favoured the Villa and they repeated a deserved 2-1 victory, a report of the scoreline from last season's Cup match between the two sides, secured by Peter 'Mac' and fellow forward Bobby Thomson. While Villa were involved in the FA Cup, Cardiff

City, who had been knocked out in the previous round, were attending to their League programme playing Plymouth Argyle. Luckily for the 'Claret and Blues,' City only managed a draw and remained one point adrift.

Monday's FA Cup draw saw the 'Villans' paired with one of the two remaining Third Division outfits, Port Vale. This was to be Villa's first-ever visit to Vale Park, but before the tie could be played there were League points to play for.

On February 6th the Villa played at home to Huddersfield Town. It was at this time that Eric Houghton's penultimate signing, 'keeper Bill Beaton, returned north of the Border to join the Airdrieonians. Beaton's sole first team appearance for the Villa, was one best forgotten - he had let six in! That was the only game he played in his first season and there were none to be had in his second. Nigel could empathise with the Scot's situation. "What I saw of him in training, he looked a really useful stopper. I couldn't be completely sure I wouldn't be dropped, but chances were I was only going to miss games through injury. Bill's situation was very much like my time at Wolves, forever playing second fiddle."

Aston Villa drew their second biggest gate of the season for the visit of Huddersfield's 'Terriers.' Thomson converted two very good chances in the first seven minutes of the game and it remained that way when the ref, blew for the interval. When the teams returned, Huddersfield let Villa know why they were so high in the table, by creating several openings. Nigel responded splendidly, showing what a great 'keeper he was. Then, ten minutes into the second-half, Thomson outpaced the opposing defence and unleashed a cracking shot into the top corner. This was Bobby Thomson's first hat-trick, and his thirteenth League goal of the season - though not unlucky for Bobby! Three goals down, the Town were far from done and made great efforts to reduce the arrears. They might have succeeded, too, but for some handiwork of Nigel's. One save in particular brought the house down when he finger-tipped a header over the bar for a corner. Gerry Hitchens scored another thanks to a long clearance by Nigel. He controlled Nigel's kick, then tore through the Huddersfield defence and rounded 'keeper Wood, slotting into an empty net. Nigel the goal-saver thus became Nigel the goal-maker; no wonder he stuck his chest out when he saw what followed his kick.

Villa were then ready to face Port Vale in the Cup tie, having collected a League point away to Leyton Orient the previous weekend. The Vale Park tie was close to being called off, after five inches of snow covered the pitch the day before. Although it had been cleared, it left huge areas of mud, which interfered with any ball skills in that section of the pitch. The home team went in at the break one goal to the good, in a half of few chances. Close to the hour mark, Hitchens levelled, though the Vale full-back claimed it was his goal. With a replay looking more and more likely, Thomson netted the winner with only six minutes of play remaining. Villa should have made the scoreline of 2-1 more emphatic - 'Mac,' Hitchens and Thomson all had goals disallowed.

The Aston lads resumed their League fixtures by welcoming Sheffield United to Villa Park. Cardiff had taken over at the top of the Division on the previous weekend, when they beat Hull at Ninian Park, taking advantage of the Villa's Cup commitments. Cardiff's 'Bluebirds' were a point ahead, having played a game extra. They had been hanging on to Villa's coat-tails since early in the campaign. When the Welsh side got the better of Leyton Orient in the capital, it became imperative Villa took maximum points. But Sheffield player and former 'Villan,' Derek Pace, hadn't read the script. He scored two in the first-half and another in the second. Credit to the Villa, they kept pegging away and were rewarded with a Thomson goal, but it was a case of 'too little, too late.' An attendance of 42,742 watched Villa slip three points off top spot.

Little Lincoln City were sitting comfortably in fifteenth position when they paid their first, and only, visit to Villa Park, where Brian Handley was handed his first Villa start. For the second time in the campaign, they denied Aston Villa the two points they needed. Nigel received a severe injury during the game, a dislocation of the left shoulder, while repelling a charge by an opponent. Stan Lynn deputised between the posts and although Nigel returned to cheers from the home supporters it was obvious to everyone that his left arm was seriously hampering him. Nigel was to sit out the next three League fixtures.

The next League game was away at Middlesbrough. Both Villa and Cardiff had played thirty-two games; City remained clear but by just two points. It was just three days on from Nigel's injury and Calcutta-born Kevin Keelan was deputising for him. Villa went out and produced possibly their best away performance of the campaign; certainly in defence, where Keelan was ably protected from the likes of Brian Clough. By beating Middlesbrough 1-0 and ending their unbeaten run at Ayresome Park, Villa kept up the pressure at the top. This result opened up a ten-point gap between Villa and next-placed Middlesbrough. It seemed to be developing into a two-horse race.

Then came some news that Nigel was half-expecting: "My good mate, Les Smith, had to retire from the game because of an ankle injury. It was a shame, you couldn't find a nicer, more down to earth lad, and 'Smithy' was a bloody good little player." Smith arrived from Wolves a month or so before Nigel followed the same route. When Mercer took over, Smith knew that his time was limited, though he was too good to be left on the sidelines. "When the current campaign started 'Smithy' had to make do with Central League football. He always hoped and expected his time would come again, but all he got was a nasty injury against Chesterfield in a Central League fixture. He was stretchered off and never played again. That injury finished him." This was at Villa Park on September 21st 1959. Now, fewer than half of the victorious Cup team from just three seasons ago were regular starters for the club.

Cup fever was running high in Aston for the visit of Preston North End for the quarter-final tie. A massive crowd of 69,732 produced record gate receipts for a Villa game played at Villa Park. With less than an hour until kick off Nigel decided he was fit to play. "I knew my shoulder was in a bad way, but I could count on the defenders to minimise what I had to face, and exactly as I said they would, they did." Nigel was determined and it would have taken a brave man to say anything different to him. 'The Villa News & Record' reported Sims or Keelan in the goalkeeper's place for the game. Perhaps the programme editor thought better than to leave him out! The side to line-up against Tom Finney and company:

Sims, Lynn, Neal, Crowe, Dugdale, Saward, MacEwan, Thomson, Hitchens, Wylie, McParland

Dugdale did a superb job of keeping Finney quiet, and, overall, Preston's play didn't match their lofty position in the table. How the scoreline was kept to just two when Villa were so fast and alert in all aspects remained a mystery. Apart from a very brief second-half spell, when North End improved, Villa were top dogs. A Hitchens' twenty-yard screamer after ten minutes gave the 'Claret and Blues' all the confidence they would need, though Preston hardly pressed. The game was made safe with twelve minutes to go when 'Packy' did, what 'Packy' did best, and made it 2-0. Aston Villa had made it to their seventeenth FA Cup Semi-Final, yet another 'Astonian' record.

Nigel missed his second game of the season for the visit of Derby County. Keelan stood in but could do little to stop County racing into a two-goal lead with a dozen minutes on the watch. A minute later Villa were finally awarded a penalty, although they should have had one before Derby's second goal. Lynn stepped up, the inevitable happened, leaving one goal in it. In a bad-tempered second-half Villa snatched victory through 'Mac' and a bullet header from Vic Crowe.

Villa's first-ever visit to Scunthorpe United's Old Showground proved to be a happy hunting trip and both points were gratefully accepted in a 2-1 win, with Gerry Hitchens hitting his twenty-seventh goal of the campaign. There were still seven League games and a Cup tie in which he could add to his collection. Even better news, Cardiff City had crashed to defeat at home to 'Pompey' 4-1. Villa were back at the summit by a single point.

Kevin Keelan produced heroic performances; in the three games in which he featured, he conceded only three goals, keeping one clean sheet; not a bad record, especially as Villa had won all three. Chances are that Kevin would feel hard done by, but there was only going to be one name in goal on the team sheet for the following weekend's semi-final. Nigel had won his fitness race against time to be back in his rightful place. "It was hard on the lad, but that's how the cookie crumbles. It was the same for me at Wolves. It didn't matter how many clean sheets I kept, as soon as Williams was fit, I was out."

Without doubt Aston Villa had to meet their most difficult opponents of the season in the semi-final tie staged locally at West Bromwich Albion's Hawthorns ground. They were to play Wolverhampton Wanderers who were second to the League leaders Tottenham and still managed by Stan Cullis. A crowd of 55,596 packed in to watch the tie with Villa fielding the same eleven that had played in each previous round. It was a game that gave neither goalkeeper much to do, due to the covering work by their defenders. Villa showed little of the togetherness that their supporters were accustomed to, and, in a game where Wolves were marginally better, it was in keeping that the match would be settled by a single goal. It came when Broadbent played in Murray, who unleashed a shot that Nigel could only parry. The loose ball was picked up by the Wolverhampton outside-left who, while Nigel was stranded on the floor, crashed the ball into the unguarded net. Last season and now this. Aston Villa had absorbed everything that teams could throw at them. They had negotiated the earlier rounds to reach the last four in the best-known knockout competition in the world. But in both seasons they didn't perform to a level that their supporters knew they could. They could easily have reached Wembley on both occasions, the hard work having been done in earlier rounds. It was Forest last year, and then Wolves, that would go on to lift the trophy again, if only.

Putting the disappointment in the Cup behind them, Villa bounced back in spectacular fashion, just four days later at home to Liverpool. Three youngsters came in as replacements; Trevor Birch, Jimmy Adam and Brian Handley. The first two had played only a combined total of thirty-five games, while Handley was just making his second start in a 'Claret and Blue' jersey. Trailing 3-0 at the interval to Liverpool, the fans might be excused for thinking that Villa's season was starting to derail. Their side had never suffered back-to-back defeats all season. Villa had started like they were going to wipe the floor with their opponents, until Liverpool, playing against a nervous defence, took the initiative. One goal followed another so that half-time was a welcome respite. "But once we got back to the dressing room, the second-half couldn't come quick enough. Mercer was in a foul mood. He had sworn before, but this was something new. He stormed out before us, shouting and screaming that we had got ourselves in the shit and we had to get ourselves out of it. Bang! He pulled the door shut behind him with such force, the stained glass panel in the door came crashing out all over the dressing room floor." Shortly after play resumed Hickson scored Liverpool's fourth. Nigel again recalls, "I picked the ball out of the net, having visions of Joe Mercer over on the side of the pitch jumping up and down out of anger in the dug-out and belting his head on the roof." It was after the hour mark when Villa pulled back their consolation, or that's what everyone thought. But then, six minutes later, Thomson halved the deficit and the Villa were now playing with their tails up. 'Mac' was upended in the area; Stan Lynn strode up to take the penalty and in it flew. Villa were now chasing the leveller. The roar around Villa Park reverberated from all four sides of the famous ground. With the supporters willing their heroes on, Thomson made himself some space, latched on to a Ron Wylie centre and scored again. "The place erupted, it was deafening. We even had a chance to win, but squandered it. When the whistle went the crowd raced onto the pitch, congratulating us all. It was like winning a Cup Final."

Even though confidence was now sky high, Villa came down to earth with a bang three days later at Charlton where they lost 2-0. The 28,068 gate was the only time that season when the Valley's attendance had topped twenty-thousand. Villa's sixth League defeat of the season came from the side they had scored eleven against at home. Villa had dropped three of the last four points available, but it wasn't all doom and gloom. While Villa had been fighting for a place at Wembley, Cardiff were being held to a draw by their bitter rivals Swansea, at the Vetch Field. When Villa played and lost at Charlton, Cardiff could have taken advantage; instead they went down at home 4-1 to Brighton & Hove Albion. The 'Astonians' had a ten-point margin over third place Rotherham, who had a game in hand.

It was March 9th 1959 and Aston Villa beat lowly Bristol

City at home, 2-1, in front of a surprisingly sparse crowd of 33,556 in a match where the hosts couldn't score from open play. Stan Lynn secured both points converting two penalties. Stan ended his season with a tally of seven goals, six of them penalties. Once again the Villa were flying high at the top of the table, but the two points from the Bristol win ensured that Villa couldn't be caught by third placed Middlesbrough, ensuring a promotion spot. At their first attempt they had recaptured their fighting spirit, emulated those old Villa legends and brought the famous Midlands' institution back to its true place in the top Division. With promotion assured, and the Championship looking likely, they had won their battle. Now they wanted to win the war. Villa still had four games to play before they could rest on their laurels. First came a visit to Ninian Park, where Cardiff assured themselves of promotion beating Villa 1-0, before a crowd of 52,364; this was by far their biggest gate of the season. The win meant the 'Bluebirds' leapfrogged Villa to occupy the top spot. Three games remained in which to try to end the season in impressive style. Two were at home, where they had dropped just five points all campaign - the first against Stoke City. Stan Lynn converted another penalty and Bobby Thomson added the second to his first season's impressive tally for the 2-1 win. When Rotherham paid their very first League visit to Villa Park, they were totally outclassed in a 3-0 Villa victory. Thomson hit a double and Wylie rounded off the scoring. Ex-Villan, Billy Myerscough, was back at Villa Park for the first time since his departure. He had a rapturous reception from the crowd and was made captain of the South Yorkshire side that day. It began to look as though like the Championship trophy was destined for Villa Park. After months of clinging to Villa's coat-tails, Cardiff City were losing their grip and failed to win any of their last games. It was of no consequence when Villa lost their last fixture in the Second Division at Plymouth, although the 3-0 loss was

140

their heaviest defeat of the campaign. In a sporting gesture, prior to kick off, Argyle's captain led his men out and formed an avenue, as the Villa team trooped on to the pitch they were greeted with tumultuous applause by one of the 'Pilgrims' biggest crowds of the season.

Before travelling to the south coast, Aston Villa had been north to Edinburgh. They had made sure of being crowned Champions on the previous Saturday, and, in accordance with an arrangement made a short time before, found themselves lining up forty-eight hours later to meet Heart of Midlothian, who were Champions in their respective Scottish Division. It was a very one-sided game and Villa had been 2-0 up, but the Scottish hosts managed to pull two back in the last fifteen minutes, saved face and earned themselves an unmerited draw.

With the season drawing to an end, Aston Villa had achieved what they had planned to do, way back in the August of '59. Gerry Hitchens and Peter McParland had notched up twenty-five goals each and Bobby Thomson wasn't far behind with twenty-two. The Villa defence was by far the meanest, not only in the Second Division, but also throughout the ninety-two teams of the League. Nigel had played in ninety-six per cent of the matches, missing only three due to his dislocated shoulder and had fifteen clean sheets to his credit.

Aston Villa were delighted to have gained promotion after only a solitary season in the Second Division. Not so happy were the Chairmen and Secretaries of the smaller sides that operated on shoestring budgets. The visits from Villa had generated far more income through record attendances but the tide of fortune had turned, and that cash cow had moved on to greener pastures!

Before the campaign had started, management had briefed players on teams, which would pose the biggest threat and stand in the way of Villa's first attempt to return to the highest order.

They had certainly done their homework; all three teams earmarked as potential contenders turned out to be just that; Cardiff, Sheffield United and Liverpool all finished in the next three positions below Villa. Incidentally, in the eight losses Villa suffered, these three sides, which required closest watching, inflicted defeats on the Villa.

Nigel and the official party left from Birmingham on May 9th for Aston Villa's post-season tour. Their destination was Sweden and then Norway with overall, a six-match schedule:

May 10th
Sweden,
Gothenburg Alliansen XI 2-1 Villa (Tindall)
May 12th
Sweden,
Helsingborg 2-3 Villa (Hitchens 2 & McParland)
May 17th
Norway,
Raufoos 1-13 Villa (Tindall 6, Hitchens 4, McParland 2 & Crowe)
May 19th
Sweden,
Bolnas 0-6 Villa (Hitchens 2, Tindall, Dixon, McParland & J Mercer)
May 24th
Norway,
Trondheim 0-6 Villa (Hitchens 4, Lee 2)
May 26th
Sweden,
Ostersund 1-7 Villa (Hitchens 2 J Mercer 3 McParland 2)

Nigel, accompanied by his two full-backs, Lynn and Neal, centre-half Dugdale and right-half Vic Crowe, started every game on the tour. Notable absentee was Pat Saward, who was on international duty with Eire. It was these mainstays of the side that had proved so important in Villa's conceding only forty-three goals in the League all season. Sims and Dugdale had played thirty-nine League games, Saward played forty, Neal and Crowe played forty-one and Lynn was ever-present. "When I first came here in '56, Stan and Peter were the established full-backs; Stan had taken over from Harry Parkes and I slotted in behind these two in place of Keith Jones. It was easy having them in front, because they were both bloody good footballers, very underrated lads. The half-back line was Crowe, Baxter and Jimmy Dugdale, who had just come in a month or so before me, and played in the centre of the park. When Vic (Crowe) got injured, Stan Crowther came in for him and Pat Saward, who had played up front, was moved back to wing-half. It was basically like that continually, apart from the last eighteen months, give or take, with Vic coming back in to his old spot when Stan was transferred to Manchester United. When you get a group of lads, who play week in and week out, you know what everyone is doing; you know when you have to move across the pitch to help out. It's no different with that same understanding with forwards; in fact, the press praise them more than they do us. Supporters don't seem to see it when it's the defenders playing above themselves, but if a forward pops up because of some neat inter-changes, well! We had no idea about records being set or anything like that. We went out and made it as difficult as we could to stop teams from hurting us. To concede forty-odd goals all season - I think we did our jobs well. But it was going to be a damn sight harder the next year, because we were going to have the best forwards in the game against us. We'd be okay."

Historians would have to go back to the side of 1937/38 to find a team that ran a tighter ship. It was that side of Biddlestone, Callaghan, Cummings, Massie, Houghton, Iverson, Broome and Starling, that, in conceding only thirty-five goals, had achieved what Aston Villa Football Club had repeated this year - promotion!

CHAPTER TEN

SPOILS OF WAR

With the previous campaign's hard-fought victory under their belt, Villa were ready to start afresh. They went into the new season having acquired only one signing, Alfie Hale, an inside-forward from Eire. Their playing squad was smaller than the one that began the Second Division campaign as eight lads had left, the majority having had no first team experience. Most of the 'Mercer's Minor's' would make an occasional appearance through the second-half of the season, players such as Aitken, Baker, Burrows, and McMorran.

Aston Villa kicked-off the 1960/61 season against Chelsea in front of a decent 44,247 gate at Villa Park. The 'Pensioners' had been very fortunate last season, finishing only three points clear from dropping out of the top- flight. That afternoon, Villa were by far the better of the two teams, with Chelsea clearing off the line a few times and their 'keeper, Peter 'The Cat' Bonetti, making some inspired saves. Aston's hot shots - McParland, Hitchens and Thomson - all picked up where they left off in the previous season, getting their names on the score sheet, earning a 3-2 victory and both points. Two days later it was a different story, as Villa went down heavily away to West Ham, 5-2. Nigel took a knock during the Upton Park clash and had to sit out the following weekend's game at Blackpool where Villa again shipped five goals, losing 5-3. Villa had been four goals down at Bloomfield Road at the interval, so to come back and score three second-half goals showed some spirit, even if there was no reward for their endeavours.

It was apparent early on that the Villa forwards were more than holding their own against the League's best in the scoring charts, finding the net eight times in three games. It was disappointing that the defence were leaking a few too many, having shipped a dozen goals in the same time, especially after their performances last year. Exactly a week after the defeat at Upton Park, Villa were able to put the record straight by making sure West Ham went back to the capital empty-handed. Hitchens was amongst the scorers for his fourth consecutive match in the 2-1 win.

Another home match followed and visitors Everton also felt the wrath of Hitchens - a double taking his tally to seven goals in only five starts. In 'The Villa News & Record,' for the visit of the 'Toffees', Nigel was congratulated on his selection for the forthcoming Football League v League of Ireland XI. It stated: 'We are particularly pleased at the selection of Nigel Sims because, during his four and a half years at Villa Park, he has performed magnificently between the posts and it is highly gratifying to know that his sterling qualities have once again been recognised by a governing body.'

The Villa would then go on to pick up only a solitary point from two away games. However Villa Park had gained the reputation in the previous season for being an unforgiving place for visitors, as they had lost only once there in all League and Cup matches. Consecutive home victories were to follow against newly promoted Cardiff City, 2-1 and, more impressively, a 3-1 win over Busby's Manchester United, in a match that saw Villa's hugely popular goalkeeper make his two-hundredth first team appearance. Nigel's record appearance meant he chalked up more games than previous Villa goalkeeping legends, such as Sam Hardy, Harry Morton and Joe Rutherford. He was now second only to the 'larger than life' Billy George.

The Aston stadium, like the good old days, was again being labelled a fortress. Villa had taken maximum points at home in all five fixtures. This resulted in the side occupying eighth position in the table, on eleven points. Burnley who were in third place were only one point better off. The club knew their away form would have to improve; one point from four away fixtures was relegation form. The following game at White Hart Lane would see Aston Villa 'assist' Tottenham Hotspur in rewriting

146

history. Villa were defeated which meant that 'Spurs' had won the first ten fixtures of their season, the only time any side had done it since the formation of the Football League. Similarly with the Blackpool fixture the previous month, Villa found themselves 'staring down a barrel', going in at the break 4-0 behind. In the second-half they were able to pull two goals back, through Jimmy MacEwan and Gerry Hitchens, but by then they had already conceded five. The game finished 6-2.

October 1960 would be an historic one for English football, but first, Villa had two more games to play, both to be staged in the shadow of the famous Aston Hall. Fans could be forgiven for thinking that the four points belonged to their 'Claret and Blue' heroes and two victories were a foregone conclusion. Villa welcomed Leicester City from the East Midlands, but through injury Nigel had to sit this one out and Kevin Keelan stood in. This could only have given the 'Foxes' more confidence knowing that Nigel wouldn't be there to be tested. The last time Villa played Leicester without Nigel, the unfortunate Bill Beaton was the stand-in, playing his only first eleven match, and being 'hit for six.' This time, Leicester City led 3-0 at the break and, though Villa rallied in the second-half, they could pull only one goal back. This proved to be Kevin Keelan's last senior game for the 'Claret and Blues;' he made only five appearances. He later went on to play over six-hundred and seventy first team games for Norwich City and collected an MBE for his services to football.

Twelve games into the new season and Newcastle United hoped to follow the example of the previous Villa Park guests. They couldn't, going home empty-handed after a 2-0 defeat to add to their other losses. Ron Wylie put one away in the first-half and Vic Crowe added the second after half-time.

By this time, the majority of League teams had floodlights installed at their grounds and winter evenings could now be exploited for 'floodlit games.' Thoughts about a new competition were aired and exchanged, perhaps with a trophy to be handed to the winners. From these ideas, the League Cup was born. Unlike the FA Cup, no Non-League sides would be included; the tournament was only open to the ninety-two members of the English League. This new era in British football had always been credited as being the brainchild of Football League secretary Alan Hardaker; but in his biography he gave the credit to Sir Stanley Rouse for the idea. A lot of clubs such as Wolves, West Brom, Arsenal, 'Spurs,' and Liverpool, refused to enter on the grounds that the competition would stir little crowd interest and they would be no better off financially. Many sides however were very positive about it. The players whose clubs participated were certainly happy with entering. "We were told before our name was entered in the draw what financial incentives were on offer for club and players alike. I was more than happy that the club had been keen to enter, so were the rest of the lads. We just took each game as it came along. The further we got, the longer we all wanted to be involved in it. The winners would receive £750, finalists £500, beaten semi-finalists £250. Players could expect £3 every match, but bonuses were starting to be serious amounts of money on top of our wages; £4 for winning the first four rounds, £8 for victory in the fifth round, the 'semi' was £20 and the final £25, with half that for a draw," Nigel recalled. He collected over £100 for his participation in that inaugural season of the Football League Cup, which would be approximately a month's wages.

On October 12th 1960, Aston Villa kicked-off their first-ever League Cup tie. They had been drawn at home to Second Division Huddersfield Town for this historic new venture. The Villa side:

Sims, Neal, Winton, Crowe, Morrall, Saward, MacEwan, Thomson, Hitchens, Wylie and Burrows

Seventeen thousand turned out to witness Aston Villa beat the 'Terriers' 4-1. Gerry Hitchens had the distinction of netting the Villa's first League Cup goal. In the third round, Preston North End awaited the 'Claret and Blues.'

League games continued, with Villa being more prolific at home as opposed to on their travels. A visit to Arsenal produced no points; then at home to their local rivals, Birmingham City, Villa put six past them; the first time they had hit them for that many since 'Blues' had changed their name from Small Heath. Hitchens wrote himself into Villa folklore, smashing a hat-trick in the 6-2 victory. Recent signing from Sunderland, Alan O'Neill, remembered it like it was yesterday, "Aye gans thru n me marra plaid a clivver baw reet to ma feet, n wee's yen up, theese anly twenty siconds on clock." Roughly translated, Alan was through and a teammate put a great ball to him, Villa were one-up after only twenty seconds! O'Neill scored Villa's fourth and was unfortunate not to emulate Hitchens and get a hat-trick. Gerry was leaving his fellow scorers behind in his wake this season, hitting twelve goals in fifteen games. In their seventh away fixture, matches which had so far reaped one solitary point, Villa made the short trip to the Hawthorns to play an Albion side only three points above safety. Doing their rivals no good at all, Villa brought the points back to Aston thanks to Hitchens and O'Neill, scoring for his second successive game. "Wor Vic borst thru n plaid a reet bonny un, Ay anly had te poke it yem." The win pushed Villa up the table to a respectable ninth. Hitchens then hit a double, against Burnley at Villa Park, bringing an eighth home win - Villa had picked up more home points than leaders 'Spurs.' The Midlanders then had to travel up to Preston for two consecutive games. Peter 'Mac' was on hand to get a point in the 1-1 League fixture. The following Tuesday a crowd of just over 7,500, down mainly due to the rain and last Saturday's uninteresting game, turned out to watch an exciting 3-3 draw in the newly-formed League Cup. Villa led this tie on three occasions.

League action saw Villa take maximum points against Fulham at Villa Park. They were now sitting in the lofty position of sixth place, with just two points separating them from a 'talent money' position.

Nearly three times the crowd that witnessed the Deepdale encounter came for the Villa Park replay where Hitchens scored his third League Cup goal in as many games - there was no stopping him. Jimmy MacEwan hit the best goal of the evening, a thirty-yard 'screamer' giving Nigel's opposite number, Fred Else in the North End goal, no chance at all.

Further victories followed, including a 5-1 mauling of Manchester City. This meant Aston Villa had gone nine League and Cup games unbeaten, an incredible sequence at this level and one that was comparable with Championship winning form. Villa were joint fifth, with Everton and Wolves second and third respectively only two points better off.

"We had no problem scoring. Well, Hitchens didn't (he had notched up twenty-one at this stage and it was only the first week of December), the other lads had slowed down somewhat, but we were still turning in good results, probably better than some of the performances suggest; but I had been on the end of hidings when actually we should have beaten sides. It all evens itself out; a season is a long time. The staff were quite relaxed about players going out and having the odd drink or two, as long as we were doing the business on the park."

A 2-0 loss over at Nottingham Forest was quickly forgotten with a Cup tie looming, two days later. Due to fog the game was put back twenty-four hours.

"We found ourselves trailing 2-0 to Plymouth Argyle at half-time. Mercer let it be known he was far from happy, what with us trailing and them being without their 'keeper for at least half of that time. 'Packy' put us back in the tie with two quick goals, but again Argyle scored. We were relieved to get the draw (3-3) and earn a replay. That's the match when young Alan O'Neill broke his foot. He was a smashing lad, Alan. No, it was his toe, I think. He joined us from Sunderland, and do you know I could hardly understand a word he said! Some of the lads thought he was foreign, from Denmark or somewhere like that! It was 'why-aye man' and everything was 'canny' and ended in 'but' and his boots were never muddy, they were 'clarty.' He always called me the 'aad man' - he thought I was ancient and I always called him the 'young un' but he wasn't much younger than me really."

Stamford Bridge was the next destination for a League fixture against a Chelsea side, sitting mid-table. "We fancied our chances in London. We had beaten them the last two seasons in Cup games and this year they had won only half of their home games. We got the win, (Villa won 4-2) but I received a strain or pull to my thigh. As I took the goal kicks it was getting tighter. I should have got one of the full-backs to take them, thinking about it after the event. I missed the coming replay!"

Fred Potter came in for the replay at Home Park due to Nigel's thigh injury. Potter had been playing and scoring from his usual inside-forward position for the Villa third team in the Birmingham & District League. During an away fixture at Lye in the November 1959, when Villa stopper Beaton was taken to hospital, Fred Potter volunteered, playing so well in goal he eventually made the position his own. He was the third man between the posts for the Villa this campaign. He gave a display of first-class goalkeeping, some of the saves deserving the word 'brilliant,' according to 'The Villa News & Record' match report. The game ended a stalemate, 0-0 but the extra-time period didn't get played. The referee decided to abandon the match at ninety minutes owing to the state of the pitch. The second replay didn't take place until nearly two months later.

Next at 'Fortress Villa' were Wolverhampton Wanderers for the traditional Christmas holiday 'derby' game. Both sides made goalkeeping changes, Sims returning for Potter and for Wolves Malcolm Finlayson replaced the injured Geoff Sidebottom. In a game that was predominantly Villa attack versus Wolves' defence, the home side were felled by two first-half attempts to which they couldn't reply. Nigel had aggravated his thigh badly during the course of the game. As expected he stood down for the Wolves' return match at Molineux forty-eight hours later. Even with Hitchens bagging two, Villa still returned empty-handed going down 3-2. Five days later, Blackpool came from the north-west and, after trailing to yet another brace from Hitchens, they fought back earning a 2-2 draw. This result kept Villa in sixth place, but Blackpool's spirited fight back saw them actually drop a position. A Bolton victory lifted the 'Trotters' up the table and Blackpool now occupied a relegation spot.

"Our home form had gone from outstanding to poor overnight - one point out of four. I know Wolves were up the top, but we had no excuses for the Blackpool match. It was hugely frustrating sitting on the sidelines knowing there was nothing I could do; but credit to young Fred Potter, he did what he had to do. My injury was hurting more than it should have, but I was told it would come right in time. I was regularly seeing the Villa physiotherapist, or more to the point, I was waiting to see him. We had to knock on the door, sit down outside his office in Trinity Road and wait to be called in. As soon as I knocked he would hurriedly pop his head out and tell me to come back later. Shortly after, you would see somebody emerge from his office and he would say something like, 'same time tomorrow' or 'see you in a fortnight.' We were the club's players going to see the club's physio and we were at the back of the queue!"

"We were starting to lose form in the League and Joe

Mercer told me I had to play in the FA Cup tie against Bristol Rovers, even though I knew I shouldn't. I could hardly walk round the house, yet here I was turning out and playing professional football for a massive club like the Villa. I could sense something wasn't right, but because I was getting told everything was OK, I just got on with it."

Gordon Lee said: "Having Nigel in goal behind you inspired you to play your own game. You would be more relaxed, you were prepared to do the things you had tried in training, because, if they failed and you lost possession to an opponent, you knew that Nigel was behind you, and his ability was second to none. He should have gone on to win caps galore. He had more of a presence in goal than even Peter Schmeichel had during his time with Manchester United and he was phenomenal."

Sims came back into the side for the Cup game at Eastville, where they faced struggling Second Division Bristol Rovers. Unfortunately for Nigel, Villa's forwards couldn't penetrate the steadfast home defence more than once despite all their possession and the game ended locked in a 1-1 draw, which meant another ninety minutes for Sims' troubled thigh to contend with. Only forty-eight hours later, Villa entertained the 'Pirates' at home. Luckily, Nigel was a mere spectator for most of the game, with the defence doing their utmost to protect their troubled 'keeper. Thomson and Hitchens were desperately unlucky not to have added more than the two goals they scored apiece. Rovers' goalie played a blinder, Radford saving his side from a double-figure defeat.

Potter was recalled to League duty for the visit of Blackburn Rovers. The Villa's early home form had definitely deserted them and Rovers managed to take a point from the game. Hitchens had scored his third League double in consecutive matches, added to his brace from the FA Cup Third Round replay against Bristol. He had found the back of the net twenty-nine times in the present campaign.

Drawn away in the FA Cup Fourth Round against the League's newly elected Peterborough United, the Villa were forced to fight tooth and nail for every ball in front of an amazing crowd at London Road of 28,266. The Villa had the ball in the net twice, with both efforts being ruled out. It was only thanks to an earlier own goal from the Posh centre-half, after a Hitchens' shot took a wicked deflection off Banham's face, that the Midlanders salvaged a 1-1 draw.

Potter faced Posh for the second time in two days when over 64,500 came out to see these Fourth Division pacesetters. United brought a massive support with them. Their club historian, Peter Lane, who has been of immense help in the researching of Peterborough United for the making of this book, was one fan who made the journey. "Posh brought close to 15,000 fans over, it was absolutely unbelievable! Two years ago, we were playing Non-League football and coming to somewhere like Villa Park to see our team just wasn't imaginable. If I remember rightly there were over 10,000 fans locked out. The most vivid recollection of the evening was the Villa fans giving our team a standing ovation at the end. Peterborough had played the best football I ever saw that night, wonderful memories!" Fortunately McParland had his shooting boots on and his brace saw off a very determined Peterborough side, who went on to clinch the Fourth Division title in their first season in the Football League.

Nigel was recalled to the first eleven on February 4th. He had missed six matches in the last month and a half. Prior to that, he had missed less than a dozen matches stretching back to his signing for the club in March '56, and it has to be remembered that he had suffered shoulder dislocations during this time.

Sims was in his regular spot, 'between the sticks' for the

match at Old Trafford. Villa took a point and had it not been for ex-Villa stopper Mike Pinner thwarting his old teammates, Villa could well have left Manchester with both points. It had taken United eighty-five minutes to breach the Aston Villa defence, through a Bobby Charlton strike. Sims had got his fingers to it, but it was just too powerful to stop.

On the weekend that Nigel was making his long-awaited comeback, Villa had dipped into the transfer market and secured from Wolverhampton Wanderers the services of up and coming 'keeper Geoff Sidebottom.

Playing for the second time in two days, Nigel came out to face Plymouth Argyle in a League Cup fourth round replay, the tie remaining undecided since mid-January. The fans could be forgiven for ignoring the game. Only 13,548 bothered turning out at Home Park to witness the hosts lose a two-goal lead. Villa then went 4-2 up, before Plymouth pulled one back to set up a thrilling finale. Hitchens grabbed his hat-trick to put the result to bed, 5-3 to the 'Villans.'

Nigel made his third start in the space of a week, when runaway League leaders, Tottenham Hotspur, came to Villa Park, which was no longer a fortress. This was a dress rehearsal of the following week's Fifth Round FA Cup tie. Lynn's converted penalty wasn't enough to secure even a point and Villa went down to 'Spurs' by the odd goal in a 2-1 loss. Villa's biggest crowd of the campaign saw latest signing Geoff Sidebottom blooded in the match. He was Villa's fourth 'keeper of the campaign. 69,672 saw the 'Claret and Blues' concede two in consecutive weeks against 'Spurs,' but with no reply this time. Villa were powerless to stop 'Spurs' progressing in the Cup which they would go on to lift at the season's end, along with the League title. Tottenham Hotspur would wrestle a record from the Villa's grasp; League and Cup 'double' winners. Villa's grip had finally been prised from this record, which they had managed to hold for sixty-four years.

Nigel would say of this new Villa signing, "I fully believe Joe Mercer and Stan Cullis came up with the Sidebottom transfer to get at me, out of spite almost. Mr Cullis never had any time for me and must have noticed how well my career was going. What with Mr Mercer getting rid of the Villa's old guard and bringing in younger players, it just seemed strange that of all the clubs Villa could have gone to for a new 'keeper, they went to Molineux."

Four days after Villa's involvement in one Cup had ended, their attention turned to another one. Sidebottom played his first League Cup tie for his new team. As in the FA Cup competition, the lads from Aston faced another Fourth Division outfit. This time, Welsh side Wrexham. Villa were too strong for them and, with Hitchens hitting two and Thomson also weighing in with one, the Midlanders progressed to the semi-finals, due to be played in April, by a convincing 3-0 score.

After sitting out two Cup ties, Nigel had to continue and missed several forthcoming League games - he was left out of the next seven fixtures. Sidebottom deputised; Villa would win only one of those games, away at Everton. Villa really were in freefall, they hadn't taken both points in any of their last seven home matches. Their form was on a par with the relegation candidates, yet remarkably they were still in eighth position, even though they had won only once in their last thirteen League fixtures.

Nigel made his long-awaited first team comeback in Lancashire for the Villa trip to Bolton Wanderers. He had been gaining match fitness through matches in the Central League, at venues as diverse as Chesterfield and Liverpool. His first game back, on Easter Monday, coincided with the debut at right-half of Jimmy McMorran. Fellow youngster Mike Kenning was notching up his third consecutive first team start. With Villa making six changes from the previous fixture, they couldn't match the experienced Wanderers and fell to a McAdams hat-trick. "I came through the match alright, my leg was still extremely sore, but I was getting used to it being like this. I honestly couldn't say if it was getting better or getting worse." Nigel's performance at Burnden Park was sufficient for him to remain in the side for the return Easter fixture against Bolton the following day. Some players weren't so lucky and more changes were made. John Sleeuwenhoek stepped in at centre-half for the crocked Dugdale, Ron Wylie was back in his more accustomed inside-forward role and Alan Deakin, an outstandingly talented youngster, came back to his favoured wing-half position, where he effectively took over from Pat Saward. The changes worked and Villa managed to take both points in a home match for the first time in eight attempts, a run lasting four months. MacEwan, helped himself to a brace, with the more frequent scorer, McParland, also getting in on the act. Alan O'Neill rounded off the scoring to make the result 4-0, with his seventh goal of the campaign. In the following game, Gerry Hitchens, who was going through a barren spell, having failed to score in his last four outings, popped up with the goal to put Villa 1-0 up against Fulham at the break. Villa eventually had to settle for a draw on the banks of the Thames where, Alan Baker another 'Mercer Minor,' would get to feature in this campaign. The result at Fulham saw the 'Claret and Blues' remain eighth in the table having won fifteen and lost fourteen. They had scored seventy-one goals and conceded sixty-nine. Not too bad for a season of consolidation, plus having the bonus of a League Cup Semi-Final, albeit away to Burnley. The players also had the added bonus of £20 if they could win the Cup tie.

"We went to Turf Moor in high spirits. We had found our touch again and had not lost in the last two games. (They had previously lost their last three). We didn't fear going to Burnley like we once had, as we had got a point up there a few weeks ago, while Geoff (Sidebottom) was having a run in the team. More importantly, we had beaten them twice in the last few years, both in the latter stages of the Cup. They probably feared us, to be honest, even though they were in the top four of the table. Alan Deakin had McIlroy 'in his pocket' for the majority of the game and full-back Gordon Lee was outstanding. Villa levelled when Hitchens sensed a backpass to stopper Blacklaw and intercepted. Villa had two penalty shouts refused and Nigel was called on only a few times, but did what was required with minimal fuss. A 1-1 draw left everything to play for in the second leg at Villa.

Aston Villa were closing down the campaign in much the same fashion as they had started - points at home, very few away. Preston came down to 'Brum' and a Thomson goal made sure Villa collected both points, but then away at Filbert Street, four days later, Leicester claimed both in a 3-1 win. Irishman Alfie Hale scored his first club goal on his debut for the 'Villans' at a ground where the Villa had struggled in recent times, suffering some big losses there. You had to go way back to 1932 to see Villa record their last win at Leicester, putting eight past them in an 8-3 victory!

Aston Villa Football Club announced at this time that they had organised a post-season tour to Russia - the team and officials would fly over in two planes, usual practice since the Munich air disaster of 1958.

Villa's last away game of the season saw them travel to Maine Road to take on mid-table Manchester City. Villa had the consolation of being the only side to score in the second-half through a Vic Crowe goal. Unfortunately, Villa had trudged off at the interval 4-0 down! Their away form had been dismal, to say the least, and had produced only four victories from a total of twenty-one matches.

Burnley came to Villa Park for the second leg of the League Cup Semi-Final, three days before the curtain fell on the last League game of the campaign. This fixture was by then far more important than the weekend match. "The only thing that concerned us was that we would be missing 'Packy' (McParland). Had his name been on the team sheet, we would have won that game before the kick-off. He bloody terrorised them!"

Villa's biggest League Cup attendance of 23,077 came to see history - hopefully written! Villa charged into a two-goal lead through Hitchens and Thomson, and Burnley looked totally uninterested at this stage. At the start of the second-half Villa's opponents came out playing like the Burnley you would anticipate. Not only did they level the tie, but during extra-time it was all the Villa defence could do to stop them snatching the goals that would take them through to meet Rotherham United in the first-ever final of the League Cup. The thirty-minute extra period couldn't separate the sides and a replay was required, to take place after the League had concluded.

The lads from Aston ended their first season back in the top-flight with a sterling performance against League runners-up, Sheffield Wednesday. Hitchens hit a double in this 4-1 demolition, his last goals before an adoring Villa Park. Gerry's goals had gone a long way to helping Villa escape from the Second Division, and this campaign he had hit a phenomenal twenty-nine League goals, more than Bobby Thomson and Peter McParland combined.

This match, from an Aston Villa sentimentalist's point of view, would never be bettered. Johnny Dixon, Aston Villa's stalwart captain took his bow before his rapturous 'Claret and Blue' followers. Had the club announced, prior to the match, that Dixon would not only play his first game of the season, but ultimately his last ever in the colours of his beloved Aston Villa, the gate would likely have doubled. Johnny made his four-hundred and thirtieth first team appearance that day, and also scored his one-hundred and forty-fourth career goal. In true Dixon fashion, giving his all for the Villa cause, he would finish the game with a broken nose. In a career that spanned sixteen years, he had played his first matches in the Football League South, before the resumption of League football after the Second World War.

As one door closes, another one opens. Unaware of these changes that day, the fans would witness Charlie Aitken make his first team debut at left-back for the Villa in his quiet, unassuming though extremely professional manner. No one would know that Charlie would go on to surpass Johnny Dixon's Villa appearances. In fact, he would end up with the most appearances of any player in the history of Aston Villa, in a career that would span the next fifteen years - two Villa legends, who between them would provide thirty unbroken years' service for their football club. Between these two would be Aston Villa's finest post-war, possibly best-ever goalkeeper Nigel Sims, who would go on to amass over three-hundred appearances.

The following Tuesday, after the nostalgia of the Sheffield Wednesday match, Villa would meet Burnley at Old Trafford in a replay, to decide who would progress to the final of the newly-formed League Cup. The Cup hadn't ignited the fans' passions as it would in later years with only 7,953 watching the match.

"We came out for the kick-off and it was like a reserve match; it certainly didn't have the feel of a Cup Semi-Final. The few fans that came looked lost on the terraces. I can't remember a first team game where I could hear the lads shouting back and forth to one another."

Stan Lynn put the Villa in front, converting the penalty won by a sandwiched Bobby Thomson. The lead was held for all of a minute, but with the game looking likely to go to extra-time, Hitchens hit his forty-second goal of the campaign to send Villa through and Burnley out. "Even after the whistle had blown and we had won, we just couldn't get too excited. We knew we were to play Rotherham United, and were very much expected to win (against a team who had nearly been relegated from the Second

Division); but when would this game take place? Nobody knew."

Aston Villa's tour to Soviet Russia went ahead as planned, with the party flying from London on the Saturday after the Old Trafford game. Hitchens and McParland were absent due to FA and international commitments. Wylie was also absent due to his phobia of flying.

Nigel played in the first game at the Central Lenin Stadium and sat out the other two, with Geoff Sidebottom deputising.

He recalled a wide player for the Russians. "They had a winger, played down the right, so he was on my left. All game he would run the line, then curl the ball in and I just kept catching it. No-one was coming for it, but he just kept doing it over and over. Later we went to Georgia to play Tbilisi, you know, the heat was incredible and the food, it was terrible. Everyone had issues with it, none of the lads thought much of the food or the place." The games played were as follows:

Thursday May 11th
Dynamo Moscow 2 Aston Villa 0

Sunday May 14th
Dynamo Tbilisi 2 Aston Villa 0

Wednesday May 17th
Moscow Combination XI 0 Aston Villa 1 (MacEwan)

Jimmy Dugdale went on record as saying he had never been as thrilled since the '57 Cup Final win as he was about the Villa's win in their final tour match of Russia. Villa had fielded only eight fit men and manager Mercer had asked the Russians for permission to play three substitutes. This was granted and the injured threesome, Sidebottom, MacEwan and Thomson, took to the pitch. Alan O'Neill remembered the Russian crowd giving the

Villa side a standing ovation as they left the pitch, due to their heroics. "They went bananas; there were tears rolling down Joe Mercer's face, he was saying, 'My boys, my boys.' Anybody who could kick a ball went out there, on the pitch, we were that desperate!"

At the end of the season Mike Kenning, who had only come into the first team in late March and full-back Doug Winton, were off to pastures new, as were Kevin Keelan and Terry Morrall. Fred Potter remained on the books but wouldn't feature in the first team again.

CHAPTER ELEVEN

MILLMOOR HERE WE COME

The new 61/62 season had already kicked-off the previous Saturday when Rotherham United and Aston Villa finally locked horns at Millmoor. It was on Tuesday August 22nd 1961, to contest the first-ever League Cup Final. Rotherham had negotiated a more difficult passage than Villa to get to the final.

Aston Villa were at a disadvantage having lost the one player more responsible than anyone else for the Midlanders being there. Gerry Hitchens, who had banged in eleven goals in just ten League Cup matches, had been sold to Italian giants Inter Milan. Nigel was not surprised to see Gerry go. "It was just a question of time before Gerry would get signed by a big Italian or Spanish side, more likely Italy, as they had been snapping up a few of the English League's top players - such as Charles, Greaves and Law - and ultimately that's where the money was. His full England debut, sometime in the summer against one of the lesser known international sides (Mexico 1961), helped put him on the road to stardom. He scored with his first kick of the match. This led to him playing other internationals; I think he scored one or two over in Italy for England; anyway he was in the shop window from then on. I don't think Gerry particularly wanted to leave the Villa. I know the board didn't want him to leave, as there would have been a big fan backlash. But they say 'money talks' and it was impossible for him and the club to turn down the offer. Villa spent some of the Hitchens' transfer money bringing Derek Dougan from Blackburn Rovers, but 'Doog' was Cup-tied and couldn't feature in the Cup Final." The number nine shirt went to youngster Ralph Brown, who made his first and only senior appearance for Aston Villa.

Harry Burrows missed the first leg but travelled north with his teammates anyway. Nigel remembered the match: "There was no special training before the match, as we hadn't long since finished all our pre-season training. It was a midweek match and we were taken up on the day of the game by coach. The game

was played home and away and it didn't feel like a Cup Final."
The Villa line-up for the first leg of the final:

Sims, Lynn, Lee, Crowe, Dugdale, Deakin, MacEwan, Thomson, Brown, Wylie and McParland.

Villa were first to seriously test their opponents stopper. After a quarter of an hour Bobby Thomson caught the ball perfectly, but the 'Millers' 'keeper, Ron Ironside, was equal to the volley. United's centre-half Madden was keeping seventeen-year-old Brown quiet. It was a dour first-half and Villa were just going through the motions. There was no spark in their build-up play and they weren't helped when centre-half Jimmy Dugdale collided accidentally with his 'man mountain' teammate Nigel Sims. The second-half sprang to life early on, when Rotherham found themselves two-up in the space of just four minutes. The outside-right, Barry Webster, scored first followed quickly by one from Alan Kirkman. The small but fanatical crowd of just over 12,000 cheered for all they were worth. The Second Division strugglers of last season had, in the blink of an eye, doubled their lead and the South Yorkshiremen thoroughly deserved it. Then Thomson was pulled down in the area and a penalty was given. The Villa fans in the crowd were already celebrating the goal, as Stan 'the wham' Lynn didn't miss these! But on that night, Ron Ironside made a name for himself. Not many goalies stopped a Lynn penalty, but he did, diving down to his left and smothering the vicious goal-bound shot. Villa failed to score, so it would be back to Villa Park in a fortnight to see who would eventually get their name on the new trophy.

The day of the second leg arrived on September 5th 1961. Torrential rain fell all day in 'Brum' and it continued for the entire match. The teams gratefully applauded the 31,201 crowd for turning out in such weather.

Villa had kicked-off their League campaign three days before the first leg and Sidebottom had been given the nod to start. Nigel came in for the Cup match and aggravated his long-standing thigh injury in that collision with Dugdale. He would be a spectator in the stand for the second leg.

The side chosen to finish the job:

Sidebottom, Neal, Lee, Crowe, Dugdale, Deakin, MacEwan, O'Neill, McParland, Thomson and Burrows.

Villa started the game at breakneck speed, determined to wipe out the two goal cushion Rotherham had from the Millmoor leg. 'Packy' McParland was guilty early on of wasting an easy chance to halve the deficit, when he fired wide with only the goalie to beat. Again the 'Millers' stopper, Ironside, came to the rescue when he kept out a Burrows' shot. Also Madden the centre-half had a lucky escape when he tried to clear a MacEwan centre, only to find the ball graze the crossbar as it went over. Rotherham managed to retain their slender lead until the break and for the start of the second period. Again they were hanging on tenaciously. A fine through-ball by Deakin put 'Packy' through, but his shot glanced off and over the bar. Finally, the home side's dominance paid off; Deakin threaded an inch-perfect ball for O'Neill to latch onto and smash into the net. With the noise still reverberating around the stadium, Harry Burrows, who had missed the first leg, burst through the Yorkshiremen's defence, beating three players and then unleashing a shot that took a deflection carrying the ball into the net. After chasing the game from the start Villa had finally hit two goals in two minutes. Although the action didn't slow down any, the ninety minutes drew to a close with no further goals, so extra-time would be played to decide the winner. At the extra-time interval, the deadlock still hadn't been broken. If the score remained the same at the final whistle, the trophy would be shared between the two clubs, each holding on to it for six months. But, with only eleven minutes remaining, Peter McParland managed to get the ball into the back of the net. 'Packy' had done it again. He repeated what he had done at Wembley four years previously - he had scored the winner in a Cup Final! "The first time we saw the trophy was on the evening at Villa Park when we were presented with it," said Harry Burrows.

Gordon Lee was the left-back in both legs of the Final and he remembered the games. "When the League Cup Final was played, us players were half and half; from the spectators' point of view and the team's, it was an uncertain adventure. The new competition had some good points, but the disappointment was, the final wasn't played at Wembley. With it being two-legged, it didn't have the same impact as a Cup final played on a big ground, just one match. When we played at Villa Park we had a big crowd, the fans got behind the guys. When you have everything to gain and nothing to lose, there's a momentum about the thing, some anticipation. We had to go forward and have a go. When we scored, the fans got behind us, and we got the result. After the Villa Park leg, we (the team) all went down to a little café in Witton. We walked down into Witton, into a café where the Villa supporters were, and had cups of tea - that was it! No big banquets or celebrations by the club." And so the League Cup was born and limped along with little pomp or ceremony.

CHAPTER TWELVE

MAKE WAY FOR THE NEW BREED

From the end of their last campaign, the signs were there for anyone of a 'Claret and Blue' persuasion to see. Villa manager, Joe Mercer, was putting greater stock in the football club's youth development plan, the greatest in their history at that point. Towards the end of the previous season, Charlie Aitken, Alan Baker, John Sleeuwenhoek, Jimmy McMorran and Mike Kenning had all been blooded in the first team. Alan Deakin and Harry Burrows had made their first start earlier in the 59/60 season and had established themselves in the following 60/61 campaign; especially Deakin, who made twenty-three appearances. Of the thirty-seven professionals on the Villa's books, no fewer than eighteen players between the ages of seventeen to twenty had played in either the senior or reserve sides. Just six of those youngsters went on to make a combined total of over one-thousand six-hundred first team appearances. The club's academy was worth its weight in gold.

Aston Villa's new campaign kicked-off at Goodison Park and featured a majority of the team that had played at the end of Villa's previous season. The most notable changes were the inclusion of Geoff Sidebottom in place of Nigel Sims, and the void that Gerry Hitchens left when he joined Italian side Internazionale. The gap was filled quickly, in an attempt to appease the fans, with Irish centre–forward Derek Dougan.
The Villa side that kicked-off the 1961/2 season:

Sidebottom, Neal, Lee, Crowe, Dugdale, Deakin, MacEwan,
Thomson, Dougan, Wylie and MacParland.

As the players emerged on the opening day, the biggest crowd in the League greeted them. Villa were grateful to their stand-in 'keeper Sidebottom and centre-half Dugdale for keeping the scoreline respectable, when in all fairness it should have been a rout. The forward line was mostly anonymous and created very little, Villa going down 2-0.

The season would unfold unpredictably. They picked up both points in their first Villa Park match, winning 3-1 against Chelsea, and then picked up a point at Molineux. Then at Mercer's old team, Sheffield United, Villa emerged with a 2-0 victory, suggesting their away form would be an improvement on the previous year. Two heavy 4-2 League defeats followed, the first at home to West Ham United and then at Blackburn. This game was remembered fondly by Villa fans as Stan 'the wham' Lynn's last game in a Villa jersey. Dougan had opened his Villa account by netting twice in the 2-2 draw at Molineux following up with a goal at Bramall Lane; but then both Dougan and Thomson were ruled out of the side for the 'Hammers' match and onwards after sustaining serious injuries in a car crash. The crash occurred after Aston Villa's League Cup Final victory on September 5th, proving fatal for their rear seat passenger, the press reporter, Malcolm Williams.

Between the two League losses came Villa's first opportunity to defend the trophy they had won eight days before! They found themselves three-up by the interval against Bradford City and looked pretty secure; in the second-half they scored a fourth within seven minutes. Then Bradford forward Webb gave the home supporters something to cheer about, when his late hat-trick put the Villa under more pressure than they would have liked. In the next home fixture Villa earned a point against Manchester United; then the home floodgates opened as the lads from Aston hit Blackpool for five. Harry Burrows was making a name for himself in front of goal scoring five in just eight games and 'Mac' had done likewise.

When the Villa were due to travel to Fulham, Nigel was back in contention. Although he had missed the opening ten matches, he had still been playing, albeit for the second string in the Central League. Fulham bagged both points in a very one-sided 3-1 win against a disappointing Villa team. Allan Jones made an appearance that day as outside-left, his only ever start in the senior eleven. Nigel was subsequently dropped for the next four League matches. "I was far from happy with the situation. I was fit and had been from the start. I played in our public trial match for the 'Blues' against fellow first team players in the 'Clarets side'; they were all handy lads - Bobby, Doog, Packy, Wylie and 'Jock' MacEwan - I pulled off some memorable saves that day. If I hadn't been fit I wouldn't have been playing for the reserves. I'd played every bloody game in the Central League and we won the lot. (He had featured in eight. Villa won seven of those and Nigel kept three clean sheets). I pulled off some bloody good saves at Fulham - the scoreline should have been much bigger! Then you know what? I was back in the 'stiffs', as the lads called the reserves. I missed the Cup match at West Ham, because, just a few days after getting back in the side, Mercer dropped me. Sidebottom wasn't in because I had played badly or because he had been outstanding, it was because my face didn't fit anymore. The manager wanted a team full of his own signings."

Six changes were made for the Villa's trip to West Ham in the League Cup Second Round. 'Mac' and Burrows both scored and the Villa were too strong for the 'Hammers' walking away with a 3-1 win.

Sidebottom started the next four League games, which included only a solitary win, at home to Sheffield Wednesday. These would be his last for the campaign, as he was demoted to Central League football for the rest of the season. Stan Lynn left the club during this period and signed for Birmingham City on October 20th. "Now there were only three of us left from the victorious Cup side of '57," Nigel lamented.

Sidebottom's last first team appearance of the season was

in another defeat away at Burnley; Mercer's men were sitting in nineteenth position, having lost twice as many games as they had won. Chelsea were rooted at the foot of the table on ten points, above them were four other teams, all on thirteen. This was only the second season that Aston Villa had been back on the 'top table,' and they didn't want to go back to second-class fare.

By the next match Nigel had reclaimed his rightful position. After his last first team match at Craven Cottage, he had been put into the reserve side where he played a full part. Villa achieved three wins and conceded one solitary goal. The young 'Villans' were challenging for the Central League title. "It got to the stage where I had made it impossible for the management to leave me out of the first team; the fans had been calling for me to be back. In Geoff Sidebottom's last two games, Villa had let in three both times. As much as Mercer didn't want me in, he had no choice."

Nigel returned on November 11th in a home game against Arsenal. They took both points with goals from McParland and Burrows, who were neck and neck in the scoring stakes. Thomson weighed in with his first goal since his return from the car accident injury. Next at Burnden Park, Joe Mercer was shown exactly what he had been missing in goal. Villa returned from the Bolton game with a hard-earned point, although the contest never reached great heights, being dominated entirely by both defences.

Quoted from 'The Villa News & Record:'
'Villa's attack had an off day, but the defence - Nigel Sims in particular - was in excellent form and usually well capable of holding Bolton's forceful attack. Sims continued to distinguish himself with a series of excellent saves - one from a hard twenty-five-yard drive by Bolton right-half Threlfall being particularly fine - he flung himself across the goalmouth and caught the ball.

In the closing stages, Bolton fought back for the decider, but Villa's defence remained firm with Sims making fine saves from hard drives by Stevens and Pilkington.'

Nigel missed the first team. "Getting back into the side was marvellous, honestly! The young Scottish full-back Charlie Aitken was playing years above himself and with Gordon Lee, a very underrated full-back on the opposite wing, I knew we would start climbing the table."

When Villa came up against Alf Ramsey's Ipswich Town they surrendered their hold on the League Cup, losing 3-2, despite Harry Burrows hitting two goals.

Winning their next three League games on the trot, gave Villa a much needed morale boost. Manchester City were neatly despatched 2-1, through goals by Harry Burrows and Peter McParland. Next, to Leicester's Filbert Street, this had become a bit of a bogey ground for the Villa, as they had lost seven and drawn two in their last nine visits. The 2-0 win therefore, with 'The Doog' scoring in his first game back since the car crash, made the game and result even more memorable. Ipswich Town were flying, sitting joint second in the table; to beat them so convincingly, 3-0, was a superb result and helped avenge the League Cup defeat somewhat. Following a 1-1 draw against Everton at Villa Park, with Thomson scoring, Villa climbed to seventh place. Villa were indebted to their defence for the result, a weaker one would have been overrun. Nigel was described in the programme as 'at his very best.' "Gordon Lee had recently come back into the side after injury, taking the unfamiliar right-back role from John Neal, who had played there since Stan 'the wham' Lynn's departure; that really helped shape the defence. Lee could read the game with his eyes shut. (Stan had also been nicknamed 'Vera' by the lads but he hated it and liked being referred to as 'Stan the wham' mostly!). Initially Gordon had come into the Villa side late last season as a left-back, to replace

Doug Winton. They had played the season out like that and then started this year just the same. Before I came back in to the senior side in November, the young Scottish lad Charlie Aitken, who had turned out for the first eleven on a dozen or so occasions, looked to have a promising future in the game. The backroom staff really rated this kid. Honestly, he had been playing regularly at left-back, firstly partnering John Neal and then Gordon. I always preferred playing behind Gordon, who I think was the better full-back. We had always played together really well; it was like we both knew exactly what each other were going to do. I can't really explain it better, but it was weird. The defence was going to get a lot tighter now, and there was a new big fair-haired lad, from the Black Country, I think. He'd come into the side in place of Jimmy Dugdale, playing in the middle, proving really hard to get past. We called him 'Tulip,' as his father had been a Dutch paratrooper or something, and we could never remember his bloody surname (Sleeuwenhoek)! Vic Crowe was always dependable playing on my right side. You know, he never put a foot wrong and never failed to put a full shift in either. Heart of a lion Vic. And then another youngster, Deakin, had taken Pat Saward's spot. He was another the backroom staff were going mad about."

Two away defeats followed, Chelsea and Cardiff, both 1-0 reversals. Nigel's performance at Stamford Bridge was commented on, with him being described as, 'again on good form.'

Third Division Crystal Palace were given the task of trying to prevent the 'Villans' progressing to the fourth round of the FA Cup. It was a seesaw match, Villa went from being one-up to trailing, before parity was restored, 2-2 at the break. In the second-half Palace took the lead once again, but as valiant as they were, they had no answers to Dougan and Burrow's later strikes, Villa winning narrowly, 4-3.

When Sheffield United paid a League visit to Villa Park, Manager Mercer's former side left with a point after a 0-0 draw, a game that truly reflected the boring scoreline.

Aston Villa suffered two League defeats, at Manchester United and West Ham, before welcoming Huddersfield Town to Birmingham for the FA Cup Fourth Round tie. It was in the Old Trafford defeat that Peter McParland bowed out, his Villa career ending and before the month was out he had signed for the Wolves. "When we played Huddersfield, we were a bit edgy, we'd left it late to see them off. I remember 'Big Pat' Saward, who was captain of the West Yorkshire side for the day, put in a good header, which I pushed over. We smiled at each other and exchanged pleasantries before we had to get ready for the corner coming over." With only seconds remaining Vic Crowe slotted in the winner, 2-1 to Villa.

Back in the League and Villa picked up their first win in seven games, with Dougan netting the only goal against his old side Blackburn. This was followed by a win over Blackpool. The 'Seasiders' were leading at half-time, but Villa came back in the second-half and took the game, 2-1. Nigel took his tally to two-hundred and fifty first team appearances in the Bloomfield Road game, an amazing number to reach. Could he go on to beat Billy George? Only he had made more appearances between the posts for the 'Claret and Blues.'

A crowd of 42,057 turned out for the fifth round of the Cup, a home game against Charlton Athletic. The Second Division outfit offered some resistance, but it was Villa who went into the hat for the quarter-final draw. Dougan and Burrows doing the damage, the 'Doog's' seventh goal of the campaign and Harry's fifteenth.

A Wednesday night home game against reigning Champions Tottenham Hotspur, saw Villa dominate the first-half so much that they received a standing ovation as they left the field. The second-half produced one or two promising raids from 'Spurs' requiring an outstanding goalkeeping performance from Nigel. 'Sims was just this with two fine saves, one a falling backwards clutch from a White 'chip,' followed up by holding a 'forty-yard hot shot by Smith', as 'The Villa News & Record' reported.

Villa Park hosted its second game in four days. Fulham were the visitors and went home empty-handed as Villa secured a 2-0 win. Villa, the only side on thirty-one points, now sat seventh in the League, and as Nigel had predicted, the defence was getting tighter. They had conceded fewer goals than anyone else in the Division.

When Villa played Sheffield Wednesday away, they suffered a heavy 3-0 defeat but this was soon forgotten as all eyes focused on the forthcoming FA Cup Quarter-Final, at White Hart Lane. By the interval, both teams had failed to score, but then Villa's hopes evaporated as 'Spurs' found the net within five minutes of the start of the second-half, and again a minute later leaving Villa trailing 2-0. For all they tried, Villa couldn't break through the 'Spurs' defence and their stopper Brown had a relatively quiet time of it. This was in striking contrast to the experience of Nigel, who was covered in mud at the close after playing one of his best and most brilliant games.

With the 'Spurs' defeat behind them, the Villa went on to play a couple of Midland derby games and the bragging rights well and truly belonged to Villa's fans after their heroes beat the Baggies at home. Then they went to St Andrews and returned with both points, after a 2-0 win against a Birmingham City side that included ex-Villa favourite Stan Lynn. It was in this game that Nigel's good friend, Jimmy Dugdale, made his final first team appearance in 'Claret and Blue' - though he wasn't to know it at the time. Harry Burrows scored in both grudge matches to cement a place in the affections of the Villa supporters. "When you played for Aston Villa, you were left in no doubt by the supporters that these games were the ones that mattered most to them. On the way to the ground they would shake your hand and pat your shoulder, wishing us all the best against our local rivals. There was a lot of pride at stake. Midlands' football matches were fiercely contested and were right up there passion wise as anywhere else in the country. Being in goal and so close to the fans behind, you could hear them almost pleading for us to beat Birmingham, or Albion, or to a lesser extent, Wolves." Burnley were the next visitors to Villa Park leaving with a very satisfactory 2-0 victory to maintain their push for the title.

In a tough, but memorable, match against Arsenal in North London, the Villa scored first through Bobby Thomson, only for half-time to arrive with the 'Claret and Blues' trailing 2-1. Further goals would see the home side increase their lead to 4-2, with Villa looking likely to return home pointless. With a 'never say die attitude,' however, the Villa rallied again and again, taking the game to Arsenal, levelling the scores at 4-4. Tommy Ewing, the Villa's Scottish forward, signed from Partick Thistle the previous month and making only his fifth appearance for his new club was then the toast of his teammates. He scored the Villa's winner, in this 5-4 classic, with just two minutes remaining!

After scoring three goals with no reply against Bolton's 'Trotters,' Villa sat firmly in sixth position. Fellow Scots, Ewing and Thomson and the Irishman Dougan, hit the goals. A small Maine Road crowd of only 18,564 greeted under-achievers Manchester City and witnessed their first win in four. The Villa side had been the more fluent movers and should have built up such an interval lead that the game should have been won. The City defence was often thrown into confusion by the clearances from Sims. Always a big kicker, he floated the ball downwind well into the City goal area, time after time.

Leicester City then made the short journey west across the Midlands, knowing that a win would put them on level points with their 'Claret and Blue' hosts. It was only down to the brilliance of Gordon Banks the England stand-in 'keeper, and some harsh refereeing decisions, that prevented the scoreline reaching greater numbers. Villa managed to score in the sixth minute through Thomson. City levelled, before Dougan restored the Villa advantage. A Bobby Thomson shot, sliced into the net by the hapless Chalmers, made it 3-1, only for Riley to convert a penalty to keep the 'Foxes' in the hunt at 3-2. Thomson crashed in a header from a Dougan centre, past Banks, to close the first-half at 4-2. Dougan, Alan Baker, with his first Villa goal, and then Burrows, all found the net in the space of five minutes. Villa were now 7-2 up! City, not surrendering reduced the deficit very slightly through forward Walsh. Villa weren't finished either and restored the margin, when Thomson hit his third of the game. The final score was more in line with Leicester's rugby side at a whopping 8-3. This was Villa's first 'double' over their East Midlands' rivals since 1931/32, when they had beaten City 3-2 on the opening day and then won at Filbert Street in January, 8-3.

When Nottingham Forest came to Birmingham they knew they were facing a highly confident side. Villa sent them back to the City Ground empty-handed beating them 5-1. Burrows scored a brace and Thomson scored for the second week running.

Villa were expecting to lose the following day, even though it was against Forest. According to Nigel, "We had noticed, looking through the match programme in the dressing room, that, since the start of March, a sequence had begun where Villa would lose a game and then win two, lose, win two. Regardless of whom it was, or if we were home or away, it made no difference. We won back-to-back matches and then lost one, three or four times in succession (it was three). So even though we had torn Nottingham, apart we weren't disappointed to lose at their ground a day later. We knew the form would continue, which meant we would win our last two games of the season, away to Ipswich Town; then the last game of the season Cardiff City, at our place."

But sequences don't run forever and Villa lost at Portman Road. Ipswich Town, managed by Alf Ramsey, would land their only Division One Championship title, preventing FA Cup winners Burnley from claiming the 'double.' As for Villa's last fixture of the season, Cardiff were held to a 2-2 draw. Dougan signed off the season with his twelfth goal of the campaign. He had been bought in to replace Hitchens, who had scored forty-two previously. Harry Burrows had exceeded all expectations by hitting twenty goals in forty-one appearances. Peter 'Mac' and Bobby Thomson also hit double figures. Even with the late high-scoring matches Villa only managed sixty-five League goals. Fourteen other sides had beaten that total. It was in defence where the improvements had been, just as Nigel had predicted back in mid-November, when he regained the 'keeper's shirt. They conceded fifty-six goals; a figure bettered only by Everton, who finished fourth, three places above the Villa.

"In a finish of stark contrasts, we were at Ipswich to see them crowned Champions after beating us and then the following week we played at home to Cardiff, who couldn't stay up!"

Aston Villa Football Club had concluded their highly satisfactory season, finishing a respectable seventh. Two days later, they went to Wiltshire playing Swindon Town at the County Ground, and winning 2-1. Then the Villa team left Birmingham to fly from London to Italy on May 15th. Their destination: Milan. When Gerry Hitchens signed for Internazionale, part of the package was for Villa to go over and play the Italian giants.

May 18th
Intenazionale 2 Villa 4 (Burrows, Dougan, Baker 2)

"At the start of the season there was me, Stan Lynn, Jimmy Dugdale and Peter McParland. It was 'Vera' and me that didn't start the first game. By the close of the season, there was me and Jimmy left, it had taken the Villa management a mere five years to demolish the side that won the FA Cup for the club for the first time in nearly forty years."

CHAPTER THIRTEEN

PLAYING ON BORROWED TIME

In the run up to the 62/3 campaign, there was a feel-good factor coursing through the veins of the club, from the boardroom to the supporters. Aston Villa had finished in the lofty position of seventh in the League, their highest placing for seven years.

Since Mercer became manager four years ago, the side had reached two 'semis,' a fifth and a sixth round, in that order, making the Villa one of the better Cup sides. Incidentally, all the sides that put the Villa out went on to Wembley and would ultimately lift the famous trophy. Villa had also won the Football League Cup in its inaugural year.

To add to the club's good fortune, they had achieved record season ticket sales and record profits due mainly to the sale of Hitchens to Internazionale. Had the club's board been more astute and invested their new-found wealth in players, they would have been able to avoid a £50,000 tax bill. But even with that hefty sum due to the taxman, everything about the club was buoyant.

Villa welcomed the new season with a home crowd of 37,657 bathing in the late summer sun. West Ham United travelled to the Midlands hoping to emulate last season's result at the famous old ground where, with Burnley, they were the only sides to achieve the double over Villa. The 'Astonians' started predominantly with the same eleven as they had used at the finish of the previous campaign which was:

Sims, Lee, Aitken, Crowe, Sleeuwenhoek, Deakin, MacEwan, Baker, Dougan, Thomson and Burrows.

Villa got off to a flyer. Dougan out-jumped the West Ham defence and headed the ball firmly home. The noise of the crowd had hardly died down when Jimmy MacEwan weaved his way through and Villa were two-up and on their way. The long kicks from Nigel caused some consternation; in fact, one of these 'space flights' allowed Dougan and Thomson to combine and put the ball in the net, only to see the goal disallowed. After the interval, Villa hit the visitors as they had in the first period, and with only twenty seconds on the clock, Thomson hit Villa's third. The 'Hammers' pulled back a consolation - but that's all it was - and Villa had a satisfactory start to the season with a 3-1 win.

Two days later, arguably the finest English club side of the time came to Villa Park. Villa had been unable to beat Tottenham Hotspur since before the war, and it appeared to be the same old story by the break, as they went in one down. Villa trudged off to a standing ovation as they had dominated for long spells of the first-half; the goal they conceded was much against the run of play. When the second-half kicked-off, over 64,000 were up on their feet; they watched Dougan climb high above the defence to head home the leveller. Within two minutes the 'Villans' had snatched a deserved lead, with the 'Doog' scoring again to win the game 2-1. The tide had turned and Aston Villa continued their winning streak at Maine Road where they inflicted a 2-0 defeat on Man City. Villa were on a roll - three games, three wins! The acid test would be at White Hart Lane, only nine days after Villa had beaten 'Spurs' at Villa Park. "It's a pity we had to face Tottenham again so soon. We were playing with a settled side, but a very young side, and it was highly likely 'Spurs' would avenge their Villa Park defeat. It would be interesting to see how the youngsters responded. 'Spurs' had gone to Ipswich's place and put five past them in the Charity Shield. They got a good result at home to our neighbours Birmingham and then we managed to 'do them' at Villa Park. They went back down to London and took it out on West Ham, thrashing them at the 'Boleyn' 6-1." 'Spurs' did get their revenge at White Hart Lane, sending Villa in at the break trailing 3-0. Villa's young side responded well, showing character, and pulled back two second-half goals through Derek Dougan and Alan Deakin, the latter scoring his second goal for the 'Claret and Blues.' The two goals proved insufficient and with Tottenham grabbing a goal in the second period, the home side ran out 4-2 winners. The following Saturday the Villa dropped a point in a 1-1 draw at home to Blackpool, but it was soon forgotten after a magnificent 2-1 victory away to Arsenal, Bobby Thomson hitting a double.

Nigel had to stand down for that Highbury match due to injury. He also missed the 4-1 reversal at Blackburn Rovers, before returning to the side on September 10th for the midweek fixture to face Arsenal at Villa Park. "I had a chat to my old teammate Billy Wright, who had taken over from George Swindin as manager of Arsenal. I wished him all the best for the season, but only after 10pm that is!" Villa were in front as early as the eleventh minute when Thomson fired in from close range. Six minutes later, there was a mix up between two 'Gunners' defenders; Burrows saw the ball reach him, swung his foot and the ball was in the back of the net in the blink of an eye. Right on the stroke of half-time Villa found themselves three-up, after MacEwan latched on to a perfect Burrows through-ball. The gap was reduced to two, as the 'Gunners' scored immediately from the kick-off. No more goals were added in the second-half. Just eight games into the new campaign and the 'Villans' had registered their first 'double.'

Nigel retained the 'keeper's shirt for Sheffield United's visit, and a special cheer was accorded him when he was made captain for the day. Sheffield had become a bit of a bogey side at Villa Park. Villa had failed to beat them since the back end of '56. This sequence stretched into another season, after the 'Blades' took both points, winning 2-1.

A reoccurrence of Nigel's thigh injury saw him sit out the next two weekend fixtures. With his fitness not being up to scratch, he was eased back into the fold, playing against Newcastle United on October 6th at St James' Park, in a Central

League fixture.

Nigel also missed the first team game the following weekend at Everton, as well as the reserves' game at home to Derby County. It was in this Villa Park fixture against the 'Rams' that Villa's stalwart centre-half and Cup winner Jimmy Dugdale bowed out. He hadn't featured for the senior team this term, but had featured in all but three of the second's fixtures. His last-ever game in the 'Claret and Blue' jersey resulted in a 1-0 victory, with the future Arsenal manager, George Graham, scoring the only goal of the game. "I wasn't to know Jimmy wouldn't play again for us, or I would definitely have gone to watch him at Villa Park. Somebody knew he was going to leave, because just a few days later he signed for Queens Park Rangers, which saddened me. It really did, it was like the end of an era. The Cup side (1957) had been totally ripped apart leaving me; the sole survivor, and I didn't expect to be there much longer. The Villa secretary, Fred Archer, lovely chap, had called me in on a few occasions and said Joe Mercer had mentioned that I was unhappy and I wanted to be away. I told him I was totally happy at this club, and I didn't have a clue what he was talking about; there was no truth in what he had been told from the team manager. Well, it started gnawing away at me a bit. I'd expected to be there for my entire career. Honestly, I did."

Nigel returned to the first eleven for the visit of Leyton Orient, but before that, Villa had negotiated the two early rounds of the League Cup, claiming big victories against Peterborough United, 6-1, and Stoke City, 3-1, both home ties; Geoff Sidebottom kept goal.

Nigel had missed six fixtures before he returned to first team action and a 1-0 win against Orient, Villa's outside-left, Harry Burrows, hitting the decider. With those two points gained, Aston Villa sat in joint fourth place in the League, level on points with Tottenham Hotspur and only two points behind leaders,

Everton.

"The youngsters were doing far better than anyone had thought they would," Nigel remembered, "To get to this position in the table we had played out of our skins. The year before we had been tagged with the label 'Mercer's Minors.' After the results we were pulling in, we were getting some major press, even being talked about as possible title contenders. Our moniker had come about after 'Busby's Babes' and 'Drake's Ducklings' of all things, because Ted Drake was manager of Chelsea. God knows who dreamt them up!"

Straight after the Orient victory, Joe Mercer told Nigel that he was back in the reserves for the following match. Nigel was seething inside about the situation. "I had come back into the side to replace Sidebottom against Orient, kept a clean sheet - what more could I have done? I was paid to stop goals and that's exactly what I did." Nigel had always gone about his job with the minimum of fuss, but playing to the best of his ability. "Maybe that's what went against me. I was never one to scream and shout and make demands, but I was certainly not getting the 'rub of the green.' I'd seen players burst angrily into the manager's office when their names had been left off the team sheet, only to see them come out all smiles, after getting themselves reinstated. That never sat easy with me, and I think it was really unprofessional."

Nigel had kept goal for the first team in eight League matches and in those eight he had conceded only ten goals. Geoff Sidebottom had played two fewer games yet conceded one more goal than Nigel, who was then dropped. He was left out not only from the senior's but also some second-string affairs. Bob Wilson, yet to make a first team appearance in the Villa goal, featured in a few Central League matches in November and December for the reserves. As it turned out, it hadn't been just the match following the Orient game that Nigel was dropped for!

During Nigel's absence, Jimmy MacEwan remembers vividly Aston Villa's visit to Hillsborough, to play Sheffield Wednesday on Saturday November 10th. "We were all back defending a corner and as the ball was delivered their centre-forward, Dave 'Bronco' Layne, caught me intentionally with his elbow, full in the face. The ref hadn't seen anything, but Charlie Aitken had witnessed it and he told him. I had to go off and have stitches in my lip. When I returned, Layne was nowhere to be seen, he had been sent off. I have a permanent reminder of that game - ever since then I have had false teeth!"

1962 was one of the harshest winters on record. Twenty-six Football League games due to be played on the last weekend of December were called off. In the first weekend of January in the New Year, traditionally FA Cup Third Round day, only five of the thirty-two scheduled ties took place - Villa's tie away at Bristol City being one of the survivors! Aston Villa didn't escape inconvenience completely; they had two December home fixtures postponed, as well as an away game at Liverpool. The Villa were unable to play a home match from mid-January to early March. On January 3rd, the FA Cup Third Round tie was played at Bristol City's Ashton Gate, ending all-square 1-1; but, due to the weather conditions, it was March 7th before the replay could take place.

When the thaw finally came, Nigel was still left out in the cold; his hopes had been raised in late February, when he had been given the number one spot for a hastily arranged match against Swansea Town - a friendly that was billed as a 'getting match practice.' He put in a first-class performance, his usual high standard, Villa won, but it wasn't enough to get him back into the first team. On the resumption of competitive football, Sidebottom was still the favoured 'keeper, with John Gavan being selected for the reserves. The Villa made an impressive start with back-to-back League wins, against Orient at Brisbane Road, 2-0, and, more importantly, in the supporters' eyes, a comprehensive 4-0 drubbing of local rivals Birmingham City at Villa Park. Inside-forward Phil Woosnam who had been signed from West Ham in November, scored not only his first Villa goal, but also in both victories.

Between the two League wins, their FA Cup run ended, going out 1-0 in the fourth round at Old Trafford, just four days after beating Bristol City 3-2 in a third round replay.

Towards the end of March, Villa travelled south to face Fulham at Craven Cottage. Sidebottom was dropped, only for John Gavan to be handed his debut. Villa lost the game 1-0 and Sidebottom was recalled. "Mercer had been telling the Villa secretary I was unhappy. If he said it again at that point in time, he wouldn't have been wrong. I was being squeezed out. Quite a few 'keepers had been tested out during my time there and each one of them failed to completely dislodge me. But now it started to feel personal. It didn't matter what I did during the training sessions, it just seemed like it didn't matter, or if I kept clean sheets, nothing made any difference."

Aston Villa then went on a run of eleven straight League defeats. They shipped twenty-seven goals during that winless streak; Sidebottom had been recalled, conceding four goals at Blackpool only to be dropped yet again. But despite his fitness and the fact that he was turning out for the reserves, it wasn't Nigel who stepped in, Mercer brought back young John Gavan.

During this time they 'couldn't even buy a win.' Now they had to play Sunderland at Villa Park in the second leg of the League Cup Semi-Final. Fortunately the first leg had been contested in the north-east in mid-January by a Villa team still familiar with winning games - the lads came away from Roker Park with a well-earned 3-1 lead. Vic Crowe scored his first of the season, along with Bobby Thomson and Derek Dougan. Villa had reached the 'semis' by winning in every previous round (which were all home ties, incidentally) and without the need for replays; but times had definitely changed. Before the Villa Park Semi-Final, the Villa supporters had witnessed their side lose 'nine on the bounce.' This was hardly form set to scare the 'Mackems' who were not only riding high in the Second Division, but had in the second round, put seven past a more than useful Oldham Athletic (Oldham would gain promotion later in the season from Division Four). Sunderland had also disposed of First Division Blackburn Rovers, 3-2 in the fifth round.

Even some die-hard 'Claret and Blue' fans had doubts that Villa could progress to a final showdown with either Bury or Birmingham City. A low attendance of 22,102 came to see if Aston Villa's slim two goal cushion would suffice. It was a game where the visitors offered nothing, not seeming to want to score, and as the home side couldn't, the match finished all-square, 0-0. It was Aston Villa who made it through to the League Cup Final, by virtue of the goals scored three months previously.

Villa were destined to meet their bitter rivals from across the city as Birmingham had defeated a very resilient Bury side, winning 3-2 in the first leg and drawing at Gigg Lane. This time the final would be played at the end of the League campaign and not at the start of the following, as happened two years before.

Finally Nigel got the nod to start his first game back in the senior side in a home fixture against Manchester City on May 8th. It had been over five and a half months since his last outing. "I thought I had actually played my last game for the club. That losing streak went on and on and it just seemed there was no way back into the side for me. The supporters at Villa Park were calling for me to be reinstated and I think Mercer thought there was a strong possibility the club might go down. It definitely would have if he didn't reverse the slide. If we had fallen through the trap door, there's no guarantee that we'd have got back out as quick as we had last time."

Aston Villa had slipped to seventeenth position and were on the same points as nineteenth placed Bolton Wanderers. More importantly, their current form was worse than most of the sides around them. If the losing sequence carried on until the end of the campaign, the club would be facing Second Division football yet again, in the space of three years.

Notable changes for the Manchester game were Nigel coming back between the sticks, and Lew Chatterley getting his second consecutive start at centre-half. Villa scored three goals before twenty-five minutes had passed - they hadn't scored this many in a match since their last win, over seven weeks ago, a 4-0 beating of Birmingham. Two of the goals were penalties; Harry Burrows converted them both after Alan Baker had put the 'Astonians' one-up. Man City scored one, but there was no way back for them. Villa snatched both points conceding only one goal for the first time in twelve League matches.

Nigel Sims was back.

A 1-0 reversal at the Hawthorns saw the 'Albion' open up a three point gap away from their near rivals. This was the last League defeat Villa would encounter this campaign. Leicester City, who were sitting in third place, were brought down to size by a 3-1 Villa victory. Dougan's goal that day was his last in a Villa shirt, and also his last appearance for the club; he would be sold to Peterborough United the following month. Three days after the 'Foxes' match, Liverpool were also sent away pointless, 'Scot' George Graham finally got to sample first team football, debuting and getting his name on the score sheet. The biggest cheer of that Saturday afternoon was the announcement that acting captain for the match was Nigel Sims. He had gone from 'zero to hero.'

Aston Villa had one more League game to fulfil before the 'Brummies' eagerly awaited Cup Final would take place. Villa went to Suffolk to play reigning League Champions, Ipswich

Town. This was just three weeks after Alf Ramsey had stepped down as their manager, to take on the top job with the national side. The 'Claret and Blues' came back with a very respectable 1-1 draw. The point meant Aston Villa had finished the League campaign in fifteenth position.

The first leg of the League Cup Final was to be played at St Andrews. A respectable crowd of 31,902 turned out to witness this 'all-Midlands affair.' Villa went in at the interval all-square, 1-1; with Bobby Thomson finding the net, after Leek had put the hosts one-up. The second-half started with the home side creating the better chances. If Sims hadn't been in splendid form, Birmingham might possibly have added to their tally. However the home side struck twice after the break, and with Villa unable to add to Thomson's early strike, the game ended in a 3-1 defeat for the 'Claret and Blue' half of the city.

Villa Park pulled in a 37,949 crowd for the second leg. Both sides marched Wembley fashion to the centre of the pitch, standing there for the playing of the National Anthem. In a game where neither 'keeper was truly tested, Birmingham came to preserve their lead and played with ten men behind the ball for long periods. Villa's frontline was unable to find a way through, failing to seize the initiative, leaving Birmingham City to get their hands on their first proper trophy!

Had the Football League not shut down for a winter period due to the horrendous weather, 'Mercer's Minors' might have been the first Villa side to win the League title since 1910. They just never got back into the swing of it when the fixtures resumed, and that, coupled with the exclusion of Nigel Sims, didn't help Villa's cause that season. "I'm pretty sure Joe Mercer was planning on pushing me out of the door and not renewing my contract when it expired in the June. But with the team staring relegation in the face, he really had no choice but to bring me back into the side, as much as he hated to do so. I was going to be there for another year!"

Nigel played in the last five matches of the campaign; in them, he conceded only four goals and kept one clean sheet. In the eleven previous matches where Nigel was excluded, Villa had conceded twenty-seven goals.

Nigel signs the match ball for Gerry Hitchens after he scored five goals in
the 11-1 demolition of Charlton Athletic.

1959/60 Division Two Champions medal.

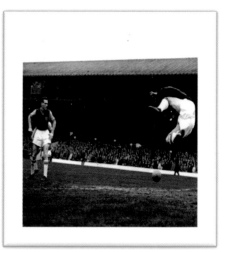

Left: Nigel at Stamford Bridge before the FA Cup 4th round in January 1960. Right: In action against his old side Wolves at The Hawthorns in the 1960 FA Cup Semi-Final.

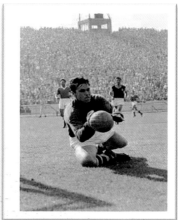

Left: Raufoss Idrettslag, Sweden 17 May 1960. Part of Villa's Sweden and Norway tour. Right: Nigel in action against Chelsea on 20 August 1960.

Stamford Bridge action.

Gerry Hitchens leaving Villa 6 July 1961.

Millmoor 22 August 1961 League Cup First-Leg Rotherham 2 Villa 0.

League Cup programme.

Winners' tankard.

Joe Mercer at a 1963 training session.

P

An Agreement made the TWENTY-FOURTH

day of .... JUNE .... 1963 between F. J. Archer

of .... Aston

Birmingham .... in the COUNTY OF .... Warwickshire

the Secretary of and acting pursuant to Resolution and Authority for and on

behalf of the .... ASTON VILLA .... **FOOTBALL CLUB**

of .... Birmingham .... (hereinafter referred to as the Club)

of the one part and .... NIGEL SIMS

of .... 52 Canterbury Road, Pen., Wolverhampton

in the COUNTY OF .... Staffordshire .... Professional Football Player

(hereinafter referred to as the Player) of the other part Whereby it is agreed

as follows :—

1. The Player hereby agrees to play in an efficient manner and to the best of his ability for the Club.

2. The Player shall attend the Club's ground or any other place decided upon by the Club for the purposes of or in connection with his training as a Player pursuant to the instructions of the Secretary, Manager, or Trainer of the Club, or of such other person, or persons as the Club may appoint. (This provision shall not apply if the Player is engaged by the Club at a weekly wage of less than One Pound or at a wage per match.)

3. The Player shall do everything necessary to get and keep himself in the best possible condition so as to render the most efficient service to the Club, and will carry out all the training and other instructions of the Club through its representative officials.

4. The Player shall observe and be subject to all the Rules, Regulations and Bye-Laws of The Football Association, and any other Association, League, or Combination of which the Club shall be a member. And this Agreement shall be subject to any action which shall be taken by The Football Association under their Rules for the suspension or termination of the Football Season, and if any such suspension or termination shall be decided upon the payment of wages shall likewise be suspended or terminated, as the case may be and in any proceedings by the Player against the Club it shall be a sufficient and complete defence and answer by and on the part of the Club that such suspension or termination hereof is due to the action of The Football Association, or any Sub-Committee thereof to whom the power may be delegated.

5. The Player shall not engage in any business or live in any place which the Directors (or Committee) of the Club may deem unsuitable.

6. Unless this Agreement has previously been determined as hereinafter provided the Player shall not before the .... 2nd may 1964
approach or entertain approaches from any other Club or person with a view to changing his Club, unless otherwise agreed by the Club and Player. Under no cir-

tion shall be cancelled by this Association where necessary. Agreements between Clubs and Players shall contain a clause showing the provision made for dealing with such disputes and for the cancelling of the Agreements and Registrations by this Association. Clubs not belonging to any League or Combination before referred to may, upon obtaining the approval of this Association, make similar regulations. Such regulations to provide for a right of appeal by either party to the County Association, or to this Association.

13.   In the event of the Club failing to fulfil the terms and conditions of this Agreement the Player may, on giving fourteen days notice to the Club, terminate this Agreement such notice to be in writing. The Player must forward a copy of the notice to The Football Association and the Club shall have the right of appeal within seven days to The Football Association, which may either dismiss such appeal, or allow the same, and, if so, on such terms and conditions as it may think fit.

14.   The following special provisions laid down by the Competitions in which the Player will compete are accepted by and will be observed by the Player:—

(1) It is hereby agreed by the player that if he shall at any time be absent from his duties by reason of sickness or injury he shall, during such absence, be entitled to receive only the difference between the weekly wage he was receiving at the time of his sickness or injury, and the amount he receives as benefit under the National Insurance Act, 1946, or The National Insurance (Industrial Injuries) Act, 1946, and for the purpose of this Clause his wages shall be deemed to accrue from day to day.

(2) If at any time during the period of this agreement the payments herein agreed shall be in excess of the payments permitted to be paid by the Club to the player in accordance with the Regulations of The Football League the payments to the player shall be the amount the Club is entitled to pay by League Regulations in force from time to time, and this Agreement shall be read and construed as if it were varied accordingly.

(3) The player agrees that he will not without the written permission of the Club grant interviews to nor write articles for newspapers or other publications nor take part in television or radio programmes and that he will submit such articles etc. to the Club for approval before allowing publication of the same.

15.   Basic Wages.

£ 50		per week from 1st July 1963		to	30th June 1964
£		per week from		to	
£		per week from		to	
£		per week from		to	
£		per week from		to	
£		per week from		to	
£		per week from		to	
£		per week from		to	

16.   Other financial provisions:—
(Fill in as required.)

£5 0s. 0d. per match appearance money when playing or on reserve for the 1st team.

Based on home match attendances, when playing or on reserve for the 1st team:

£1 0s. 0d. per 1,000 on any excess of 32,000 up to 50,000
£2 0s. 0d. per 1,000 on any excess of 50,000

When playing or on reserve for the 1st team in away matches, payments will be based on last home match attendance.

17. Any other provisions:—
   (Fill in as required.)

18. In consideration of the observance by the said Player of the terms, provisions and conditions of this Agreement, the said   F. J. Archer
on behalf of the Club shall pay to the said Player the wages, bonuses and fees as determined hereinbefore and this Agreement (subject to the Rules of The Football Association) shall cease and determine on   30th June 1964   unless the same shall have been previously determined in accordance with the provisions hereinbefore set out. On such determination, and provided that this Agreement is not for a period of one calendar month only the Club may (but subject always to the right of The Football Association to refuse such retention of its own motion) retain (subject to the Rules of the Competition in which the Club competes) the Player in accordance with the Rules of The Football Association provided that the Club is willing to offer the Player suitable terms (both as to remuneration and otherwise) in accordance with such Rules and that notice to this effect is given to the Player not later than   2nd May 1964

As Witness the hands of the said parties the day and year first aforesaid

Signed by the said   F. J. Archer

                and

                NIGEL SIMS   10 Sims

                                                                    (Player)

in the presence of

(Signature)   S. Allcock

(Occupation)   Clerk, Aston Villa F.C.,

(Address)   Trinity Road, Aston,   (Secretary)

               Birmingham, 6.

Toronto City FC 1964/5.

Home in Toronto and (right) the Varsity Stadium, Toronto.

Canadian All-Star Representative XI v Italian Representative XI.

Nigel at London Road and lining up with his new teammates.

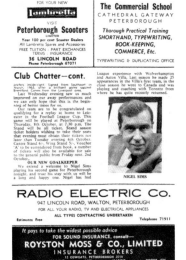

Left: Nigel's debut for Posh away at Luton Town Right: Piece in Peterborough United v Brentford programme welcoming Nigel… 28 September 1964 (home debut).

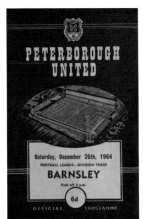

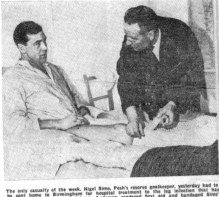

Programmes for Nigel's last home and away matches for "Posh." In the middle Nigel is laid-up in bed while at Peterborough.

Top: Upper Canada College crest, Toronto Falcons programme and crest.
Bottom: The prestigious Upper Canada College where Nigel taught.

Toronto Italia 1967...Nigel during his second spell in Canada in 1967.

Nigel with Marjorie.

Nigel and Marjorie in Switzerland.

With Marjorie.

With family friend Sofie (left) and daughter Deborah.

It never stops....

Trying his new gloves for size.

With Marjorie.
Wright.

With ex-teammate Billy

Peter McParland, Randy Lerner, Jackie Sewell and Nigel. A trio of 57 winners. Guests of Randy Lerner at the FA Cup 3rd Round tie versus Manchester United.

With author Colin.

Caricature kindly donated by Norman Hood. Nigel is one of Norman's three
all-time favourite players.

CHAPTER FOURTEEN

AND THEN THERE WERE NONE

On June 24th 1963 Nigel Sims was summoned to the inner sanctum of the Trinity Road Stand to put pen to paper on what would be his last Aston Villa contract. "I was upstairs in Fred Archer's office, he was the club secretary. The season had finished just a month before and Fred said to me that he and the board had been extremely concerned at the peril at the end of last season and the distinct possibility that Aston Villa could get relegated. He also brought up the fans' unrest and how they had been repeatedly calling my name from the terraces, something I hadn't known about because I was in the reserves side. The Board of Directors had found Joe Mercer very uncooperative when they mentioned having me back in the side and Fred implied that they had to put pressure on the manager to reinstate me before it was too late. Apparently the subject had been broached between Joe and the Board a while before I was brought back, but they hadn't been persuasive enough. Fred said the Board owed me a huge debt of gratitude because they thought I had done as much as anyone else keeping the club up. I was pleased to sign the new contract, but in the back of my mind I knew I would be playing under someone who didn't want me there. Fred could see now for himself, by my willingness to sign, that I hadn't been unhappy at the club at all, or asked to leave like he'd been told."

With the new campaign ahead changes were taking place. Gerry Hitchens replacement, the 'Doog,' was never quite able to fill his boots, so the Derek Dougan sideshow moved down two Divisions to newly-promoted Peterborough United. Hitchens had scored more than twenty-six goals in just thirty-one games during his last season at the club. 'Doog' never lived up to that and had taken two seasons to notch up the same number.

Aston Villa's latest goal getter was Tony Hateley, a prolific scorer from Notts County, who hit seventy-seven goals in just one-hundred and thirty-three appearances. County fans revered him, as it was Hateley's goals that enabled the 'Magpies' to gain promotion to Division Three. "I remember playing a friendly against Northampton Town. It was one of Hateley's first games and he scored a few times in what was a big (7-0) win for Villa, (it was actually his second, as he had starred for Villa against Shrewsbury Town three days previously, but failed to find the net) and he carried himself very well. There were goals in that lad."

When Villa kicked-off their campaign opener at Nottingham Forest, Tony Hateley received more than his share of the attention. Until recently he had plied his trade with Forest's rivals County, whose ground, Meadow Lane, was within spitting distance of the City Ground just across the River Trent. He fired the only goal of the game, which added a bit more intensity to the atmosphere. The winner came via a long Nigel Sims kick, which deceived the Forest defenders and gave Hateley the easy task of stroking the ball home, off the foot of the post. "It was very satisfying to get a good start to the season. The supporters didn't realise just how important a winning start was for the players. It was the first time since I had been at the club that we'd been on the winning side at Forest. They never gave much away to the Villa and it was great to make the goal for Tony as well."

Two successive home defeats against fellow League founder members, Stoke and Blackburn, came as a shock to the Villa faithful, especially after that promising victory on the first day of the season. A second goal for Tony Hateley in as many games had the Villa faithful hoping they'd finally found a suitable replacement for Gerry Hitchens. Villa met Stoke City for the second time in nine days. At their Victoria Ground, and in a worthy display, Villa returned to the Midlands with a share of the spoils. A convincing win at Blackpool saw Harry Burrows record his first-ever and only Aston Villa hat-trick.

As early as it was into the campaign, Villa supporters were

looking through their record books. Aston Villa remained unbeaten away, but had failed to pick up anything in their two home games against what could be best described as 'middle of the table' opposition. Traditionally, the Villa had struggled on their travels but had a reputation for taking no prisoners at Villa Park. Until now, their current form was a complete reversal. However, 'normal service was resumed' when Villa travelled to North London, to take on Arsenal. The home side won by three clear goals, with Villa unable to find a way through a well-disciplined 'Gunners' defence. This was Bobby Thomson's last appearance in a Villa shirt; three weeks later he had signed for Birmingham City.

Chelsea were the next side to visit Villa Park and they knew that, the 'Villans' were struggling for home form, they would give it their all. Unfortunately, they were to visit on a day when a 'superlative Nigel Sims denied them goals,' as described in 'The Villa News & Record.' Jimmy MacEwan played his first game since March '63 and celebrated stylishly by bagging the game's opener. Tony Hateley did what the Villa signed him to do, and netted his fourth 'Claret and Blue' goal in seven outings. Chelsea's rivals, Tottenham Hotspur, followed the 'Pensioners' to Villa Park and fared, much better, putting four past the 'Villans.' Villa were leading at the break from an own-goal by 'Spurs' right-back, Baker. The final score was 4-2, with Villa's inside-forward Alan Baker also getting on the score sheet.

Aston Villa's next fixture took them back to the capital, where they played their fourth London-based side in a row, away at West Ham United. A Harry Burrows' goal was responsible for helping his side secure their first-ever League win at Upton Park. The men from Aston sat twelfth in the table and seven of their nine points had come from their away travels.

For Nigel it was like old times. He started the season as first choice in goal, although he didn't know if there was some boardroom intervention at work there. With nine consecutive League games under his 'Claret and Blue' belt, things were going well.

Barnsley were the first hurdle for the 'Astonians' in their pursuit of the trophy that they were so close to landing last season - the Football League Cup. Third Division Barnsley played well above their standing that night, although Villa should have added more emphatically to the eventual 3-1 scoreline. All down to a mixture of bad misses by their forwards and the Barnsley stopper having a match to remember!

Four defeats followed, with Villa recording a somewhat unfortunate loss in a 5-2 drubbing at Liverpool's Anfield. Although the home side had raced into a two-goal lead after only fifteen minutes, the Villa rallied and were able to halve the deficit when Hateley turned brilliantly and shot into the net. With half-time looming, 'Big Tony' managed to out climb the 'Reds' defence and nodded home the equaliser from a corner kick. Villa went in at the interval all-square, having come back from two-down. Not many sides could claim to have done that at Anfield. After half-time there was still a lot of football to be played, as it turned out it was all at the wrong end, Villa shipped three more to lose 5-2 by the final whistle. Tony Hateley had found the net three times in that ill-fated four-match sequence of defeats. "After all those defeats, I got a phone call from the manager of Southern League outfit Nuneaton Borough. Joe Mercer had given him my home phone number and said that I had been telling the lads that I had a desire to play for Nuneaton, as they were my local side. I told him I was signed on contract for Aston Villa and thanks, but no thanks. I told him that somebody was lacking in geographical skills as I was from Derbyshire, not Warwickshire! Then I wondered how long it would be before Fred Archer, the club secretary, would come looking for me to ask what was happening and why was I unhappy."

On October 16th, West Ham travelled to the Midlands for a League Cup Third Round tie, seeking revenge for the 'Villans' having taken both points in the recent League game on their patch. Villa's play was as poor as the attendance, which was a disappointing 11,194. The visitors gratefully accepted the two goals they were gifted and with that the Villa's interest in the League Cup ended for another year.

The next Villa Park encounter saw the home side show a bit more backbone when they played hosts to the Arsenal. By the break Villa were trailing by a single goal. Remembering what had happened recently on Merseyside and how games could change in moments, Villa came out for the second period, took the bit between their teeth, and totally dominated proceedings getting their just rewards when Tommy Ewing was upended. Tony Hateley took responsibility and coolly slotted home the penalty. With the noise of the home crowd backing the players to the hilt, Villa swept forward repeatedly. The winner finally came when a perfectly-flighted Burrows' cross was latched on to by Villa's new found goal-scoring machine Tony Hateley.

Villa's next away day was a visit to Hillsborough. They returned empty-handed after being blatantly robbed in a 1-0 defeat at the hands of Sheffield Wednesday. The Wednesday goal was so far offside everybody in the ground could see it, with the exception of the referee and his officials. Perhaps the Villa players remonstrated too vehemently, as later in the match; Harry Burrows' 'legitimate' goal was chalked off - for offside! The game was more fondly remembered by anyone of 'Claret and Blue' persuasion for Dave Poutney, who played a blinder on his debut at half-back.

Once again the tide was to turn and although Villa were struggling at the away grounds, they were starting to pick up the pace at home.

When Bolton Wanderers came knocking, they were

dispatched, defeated from 'Fortress Villa,' 3-0 with Harry Burrows helping himself to a couple. Then Craven Cottage witnessed the Villa go down 2-0 to Fulham the following week.

When Nigel's leg injury reoccurred, he was unable to participate in the Villa's home game against highflying Manchester United. They were third in the table while Villa were sitting quite a bit lower in nineteenth. Vic Crowe was also injured, so Alan Deakin was brought into the wing-half berth. Within thirty-five seconds Tony Hateley had put the 'Villans' one-up! This inspired the Villa and, before twenty minutes had been played, Deakin had doubled their lead. Deakin and MacEwan were taking the game to United.

Harry Burrows recalls what happened next: "With ten or so minutes to go before the break, Alan on the right side, slid in and won the ball from United's inside-left Denis Law. It was a fair tackle, but it made Law look a bit silly. Law quickly turned, came over to where Alan was lay, still on the ground, it all happened so quick, and kicked him really viciously. Straight away the fans were furious, shouting and screaming. The ref sent him off immediately. As he got close to the side of the pitch it looked like it was going to get ugly. It appeared that Denis Law had mouthed off at the supporters who were heckling him. Policemen came across and escorted Law away from the playing area and to the tunnel. We were told later that the police had insisted he left the ground before the final whistle, for his own safety." Two-nil up and playing against ten men, Villa took advantage of having that extra man, playing in the space, down the channels, soon increasing their lead, with Hateley hitting his second of the match. Burrows rounded off a morale boosting result by striking home one of his trademark left foot shots-4-0 to Villa. Nigel was also out for the trip to Turf Moor, where Burnley beat the 'Claret and Blues' 2-0, registering their seventeenth consecutive League game without defeat against the Midlanders.

By November 30th, Nigel was back to fitness and selected to play in the first eleven. For the next two matches, at home to Ipswich Town and away to Leicester City, he kept clean sheets, both games ending in 0-0 draws. Villa were unable to capitalise on these impressive defensive displays by scoring at the other end, and had to settle for a single point from each match. Shooting form improved in time for the visit of Nottingham Forest, who were neatly dispatched 3-0, Nigel being given little in the way of trouble. Burrows and MacEwan were joined on the score sheet, by the unfortunate Forest wing-half Whitefoot. This put Harry Burrows on ten goals, two short of leading scorer Tony Hateley.

Two successive away fixtures then yielded just a single point. Blackburn took both points in their 2-0 win at Ewood Park. A Boxing Day encounter against Nigel's old side Wolverhampton Wanderers followed. It was a 'game of two halves.' Although it was a goalless at the interval, the Villa should have gone in with a commanding lead, already certain of the points. After half-time the home side gleefully took advantage of defensive mistakes and the 'Claret and Blues' were 3-0 down only six minutes after the restart. Then came the counter-attack. Poutney scored his first goal in the club's colours starting the ball rolling. Vic Crowe notched his only goal of the campaign, then that man, Tony Hateley, secured the Villa a share of the spoils. "This game, just as the first-half at Anfield had done, totally summed up the character Villa had in the side," Nigel recalled. Just forty-eight hours later Wolves made the short trip to Aston for the return fixture of the 'Festive Period.' The visitors had the Villa chasing an equaliser from the sixteenth minute, which came when Burrows levelled after ramming the ball home from a clever Ewing centre. In the second-half Wolves again managed to get their noses in front, only for Burrows to score his second of the match to bring Villa back on equal terms. After trailing in both of the Wolves matches, three times, Villa had clawed it back three times!

Aldershot came to Villa Park in the first week of January to contest the FA Cup Third Round. In front of over 21,000, the Fourth Division side played with resilience, certainly none more so than their 'keeper Jones. Their play certainly belied their Football League standing. Nigel remembered how tough the game against the minnows had been. "We were bloody fortunate to still be in the tie," the match ended 0-0. "After the game, Nuneaton's manager phoned me again and asked if I would consider coming to play for his side. He said they could put together an attractive package to get me there, as someone of my stature would put another thousand on the gate. I informed him, yet again, that I was under contract to Aston Villa. After a slight pause this chap replied, 'not for long,' and then he put the phone down. I thought it was a strange thing for him to be saying."

The replay saw a crowd of 13,566 flock to Aldershot's compact Recreation Ground. The home supporters could sense a possible giant killing was on the cards. The 'Shots' didn't disappoint their home followers and with everything to gain and nothing to lose, they strove forward. Aldershot scored twice and though Hateley pulled one back for the visitors, it was a case of 'too little, too late!' Aldershot had beaten Aston Villa 2-1. The first time Villa had been knocked out in an FA Cup tie by a team playing in the League's basement Division.

With twenty-five games gone Villa were in seventeenth position, though they were more or less safe having an eight-point lead over relegation placed teams Ipswich Town and Bolton Wanderers, who were points adrift of safety, and both teams would drop through the trapdoor at the end of the season. Ipswich had won the First Division title only two seasons previously.

Back in the League, and Nigel turned out at Villa Park as

captain for the day, to keep goal against Blackpool. He didn't know it at the time, but this would be his last home game in the Villa jersey. He played his part in ensuring Aston Villa kept up their impressive home record with a fine 3-1 victory. That afternoon Villa achieved only their second double of the season, also beating Nottingham Forest home and away earlier in the campaign.

On January 18th 1964 at Aston Villa's away fixture at Stamford Bridge, Nigel Sims made his last ever appearance for Aston Villa Football Club. It was the club he had given blood sweat and tears for, over the last eight years. He had racked up three hundred and ten first team, League and Cup appearances in his time. Villa played well enough that afternoon in icy conditions to have earned at least a point despite a 1-0 defeat. It was the Chelsea 'keeper, John Dunn, who later signed for the Villa, most called upon out of the two 'keepers. Nigel bowed out without actually knowing it.

Subsequently dropped for the forthcoming League games that Villa failed to win, Nigel didn't even make the Central League's reserve side. The emerging talent of 'Brummie' Bob Wilson had secured that place.

Aston Villa secretary Fred Archer summoned Nigel to his office after a Villa Park training session. Nigel was expecting to hear that the Board would see to it that he would be reinstated to the first team as soon as possible or perhaps even better; the club were going to give Nigel a testimonial, just as they had granted Vic Crowe earlier in the season. He couldn't have been further from the truth. "Fred could hardly bring himself to look at me. He then told me in a tone I didn't recognise as being Fred, that, due to my sterling services to Aston Villa Football Club, they were letting me go on a free transfer. I was flabbergasted; honestly I was stuck for words. What would I do? Where would I go? Aston Villa was a huge club; I was settled in the area. The fans were great, the set-up was first class, we stopped at the finest places, nothing was too much trouble. The players, well they were a great set of lads, we were like a family, I couldn't comprehend what was happening. I was being told to walk away from Aston Villa, and I was devastated. Joe Mercer had finally got his wish. Now of course, the calls from the Nuneaton manager, and especially his little quip about 'not for long', all made sense. This had been coming for a while and I just hadn't seen it. I was hurt, I was angry, but most of all, I was extremely disappointed to have been treated like that by such a fine club. I had given it my all from the moment I got there. All those times I turned out with my thigh heavily strapped; I would finish the match in agony and I would have this bloody big tube inserted into my thigh to drain off all this fluid that had built up during the game. In 2008, when I went to see my consultant it emerged that this persistent thigh injury was actually due to having broken my hip. He asked me when I had broken it. Well I told him that I hadn't, and he said, 'Yes you have and what's more, because the way the bone has knitted, it's obvious that this happened many, many years ago'."

In a campaign of stark contrasts, Villa had started the season with title-winning form on their travels; in their first five away fixtures the men from Aston had tasted defeat only once, winning three and drawing the remaining one. They had taken more points on their travels than at Villa Park, where they had won once and lost five. As the season unfurled, their home record would invariably get stronger while they failed to register another away victory during the entire campaign.

After Nigel's departure, Geoff Sidebottom started the first half-dozen fixtures. In the sixth match he conceded four goals in the defeat at Everton in a match played on the Friday night, due to Liverpool playing the following day (February 28th, the night the author came into this world kicking and screaming, it has always been said because the Villa had lost!) Sidebottom was subsequently dropped, losing his place for the rest of the season to youngster Robert (Bob) Wilson who played in all remaining nine matches. Wilson never featured in the first team again after that.

CHAPTER FIFTEEN

CANADA, A NEW FRONTIER

Nigel had played his last game for Aston Villa and now he needed to decide where he wanted his career to go. Nuneaton Borough was not on the cards.

News travelled fast even in those pre-mobile phone days. Bob Pemberton was a former sports journalist for the Daily Mail; he had vaguely known Nigel before emigrating to Canada. Nigel and Bob shared a mutual respect for each other and were both highly respected in their chosen fields. When Bob heard that Nigel and Aston Villa had parted company, he got in touch with some old journalist acquaintances and asked them to track Nigel down and sound him out on the possibility of his playing 'soccer' in a relatively new Canadian League. Although the Canadian League was fairly young, it had gathered momentum at an astonishing pace in just a few years.

The newly-created Eastern Canada Professional Soccer League, to give it its full title, was the brainchild of two highly-regarded, influential men, George Gross and Peter Bosa. Gross was a sports journalist and winner of the prestigious Elmer Ferguson Memorial Award. (Given 'in recognition of distinguished members of the newspaper profession whose words have brought honour to journalism and to hockey'). Bosa was an insurance executive and politician who later rose to be a Senator. In 1960, over the Christmas period, their sporting idea was born. Bosa had friends in Hamilton and they were interested in forming a professional football team, on the condition that Gross and Bosa could come up with three more teams, two from Toronto and one from Montreal. Bosa had the backing of his executive, to bring the Italia team from the National Soccer League. Gross instructed an associate, Dr. Ernest Stastny, to sort out the Montreal side, while he would set about building the second Toronto team. Gross turned to Macedonian-Canadian businessman and soccer fanatic Steve Stavro, journalist Ed Fitkin and industrialist Larry Myslivec and between them they formed Toronto City. Stavro was a wealthy man with a 'grocery empire' and his wealth would bankroll the venture.

In early 1961 Gross, accompanied by Fitkin, flew to England. Their mission, recruit a few players to feature in their newly-formed League during the English League's summer shut down. They took the football world by storm, attracting notable international stars such as Johnny Haynes, Stanley Matthews, Danny Blanchflower and fellow Scottish internationals Jackie Mudie, Blackpool's centre-forward and Liverpool 'keeper Tommy Younger.

The ECPSL season kicked-off in the spring of 1961. Less than a week after the League's opening match, came the eagerly-awaited clash between Toronto City and Toronto Italia at the Varsity Stadium, in front of a sizeable crowd. The local rag, the 'Globe and Mail' ran the headline: 'Watch It, Chaps, Here Comes Soccer.'

Tommy Younger, who later went on to be a director and then chairman at Hibernian FC, gained his first coaching role during this period. It was also at Toronto City that the English, Scottish and Northern Irish captains played on the same side for the last time.

Attendances for the first season (1961) were far better in Toronto than the other participating cities. The Varsity Stadium admission prices were $1.50. But figures for Montreal and Hamilton were far less than had been expected. The following two seasons were more or less on par with the League's first year and an increase in ticket prices saw a sharp decline in attendance figures for the 1964 summer campaign. That had to have a knock on effect on players; there would be fewer foreign stars willing to come over to play in the ECPSL in future campaigns. This situation wasn't to the supporters' liking; prices were going up and instead of watching the top professionals from foreign countries they had to make do with watching second-rate, homegrown footballers. It was a death sentence for the ECPSL.

Toronto City Soccer Club was the one to attract Nigel's attention. He made the journey 'across the pond' in April 1964, after his Villa contract was terminated in mid-February. The big names from two years ago had long gone, but there were still plenty of familiar faces to see when Nigel arrived. The big surprise was that the up and coming, former Non-League Bath City boss, Malcolm Allison, had recently taken the manager's job at Toronto. His job was not just to turn Toronto City into a better footballing side, (they finished fifth in a League of five teams in the previous season) but was also to tap into and play up the rivalry between the British-supported City team and their Italian rivals, Toronto Italia and Toronto Inter-Roma.

He had taken Bath to a highly respectable third-place finish in the English Southern League turning a few heads before going out of the FA Cup in a third round replay against Lancashire giants Bolton Wanderers. It was his record at Bath that had alerted clubs globally.

'Big Mal' inherited Walter Chyzowych, the Ukrainian forward, who set goal scoring records in his time at Temple University in the United States. Chyzowych had been at Toronto City since their inaugural year of '61. Combining the inherited players with the acquisitions he brought over from the UK, 'Big Mal' was able to assemble a good squad. Nigel Sims was one of a number of players who had been brought in ready for the forthcoming campaign. There was also the Brazilian midfield maestro Alex Ely, who was coaxed back into the game during the ASL (American Soccer League) 'off season', in both 1961 and '62. Alex had previously starred for arch-rivals Toronto Roma. From 'back home,' Allison also recruited Ted Purdon, Charlie Fleming, Johnny Brooks and Norman Sykes. Ted was an inside/centre-forward and was better known for his stints at Birmingham City and Sunderland. Charlie, formerly of Sunderland, was now playing his football for 'Big Mal's old side, Bath City. Johnny was a former England international, but had started his career with his home team Reading. An inside-forward, he would play the remainder of his football in the capital with spells at Tottenham Hotspur, Chelsea, Brentford, and half a dozen games for Crystal Palace, before heading to Canada. Norman was well-known to Allison after plying his trade in the West Country for Bristol Rovers. He was a wing-half who went over to Canada to use the time as a rehabilitation exercise to aid with his problematic arthritic hip. Norman would leave Toronto City after the end of the summer season following Malcolm to Plymouth Argyle.

Nigel and his fellow 'Brits' settled very quickly into their new surroundings - nice modern apartments in the Frontenac Arms Hotel, Central Downtown Toronto. Training sessions were carried out twice daily at the Varsity Stadium, where the team played their home games. As it happened, all three Toronto sides; City, Italia and Inter-Roma, played their home matches at the Varsity. Being a vast country, away matches usually involved plane flights, but more often than not it was a case of there and back on the day of the game.

There was a late addition to the squad when Tony Book, former Bath City Captain and colleague of Big Mal joined the rest of the British expats. Nigel remembered, "Tony started his football career as an inside-forward, when he was just a youngster, then he had been converted to a full-back. Ultimately he had never played above Non-League level and when Malcolm brought him over, Tony came direct from the building site. He was a brickie."

The Eastern Canadian Professional Soccer League was made up of five teams; Toronto City, Toronto Italia, Toronto Inter-Roma, Montreal Italia and Hamilton Steelers. Each side played twenty-four games in the League meeting each other six times, three games at home and three away. All Toronto sides playing at

Montreal or Hamilton flew out on the morning of the match and returned the same day. Two points were awarded for a win, one for the draw, or tie, as they called it over there. Nigel had some good memories from his Canadian days. "Honestly, most of the players like me had been expecting to come over, play a bit of football and have a summer holiday really! On the first day Allison said, "Come on, we'll get fit and we'll bloody enjoy it." You know, that summer the extra training he put us through really paid off, my fitness levels and conditioning were as good as they had ever been and I was well into my thirties by then. Malcolm took his job very seriously, he took total control, everything was done like he was running a title winning team back home. I admired and respected him as a coach and as a man." Some of the antics put a smile on Nigel's face. "When we were playing a match against one of the Italian-supported sides, Malcolm insisted that as well as the opposition, we wind up their fans also. The teams would normally wave to all sides of the stadium prior to kick-off, but Malcolm told us to purposely ignore where our opponents fans were standing. That caused a bit of an atmosphere, to start with, but then, when we scored, Malcolm had us wave at their section. When that happened, the place erupted, boy, did they react! If he'd said to do the same at a Villa versus Birmingham City 'derby' game, he would have been arrested for having caused a full-scale riot. The owner Stavro, who wanted to cause animosity between the British and Italians, couldn't have been more pleased and I don't think he would have found anyone that could have done a better job than Malcolm."

Tony Book had some good memories from his time in Canada. "I'd come over after playing Non-League and there were these well-known footballers, some internationals, who I'd read about in newspapers and now I had them playing alongside me. I'd been on fifteen quid a week at Bath. In Canada I was on twenty, which was probably less than the others, but they were all well-known pros. We had nice digs, and I had an old mate I had known from my time at Bath. He'd emigrated to Canada, to work at a record label and would call at the hotel a few times a week and some of us English lads would go out for a meal with him. We trained daily at the Varsity Stadium and always managed to fit in a game of 'head tennis.' It was at these sessions where we would meet up with the local lads from the team, as they didn't live with us at the hotel."

After just a few months of being in charge at Toronto, Malcolm Allison shocked his team when he returned to England to manage Plymouth Argyle. The 'Pilgrims' board had been impressed with his achievements in the West Country at Non-League Bath City, and his interview at the Savoy Hotel the day before he flew to Canada had obviously worked in Malcolm's favour. It had been a three-way contest for the Argyle post, with Allison up against former Aston Villa players Frank Broome and Eric Houghton. "He asked me and Tony to follow him" said Nigel. "We stayed until the end of the football season in Canada when Tony was voted the best defender in the Eastern Canadian Professional Soccer League. Then we were selected to play for a Canadian XI against an Italian League XI in a representative one-off match."

"Malcolm was certainly a very good man manager. He could 'eke the last drop' out of anyone. No-one was surprised when he went on to achieve what he did in the game. It's just a pity he hadn't stayed with us a bit longer to see the team that he had a big hand in building, win their only ever Championship."

At the fourth time of trying Toronto City managed to finish top of the pile after losing in the semi-final in their first season and then reaching but losing the final in their second year.

"We had an enjoyable time; we lost only four games in the season. As well as winning the League title we won the play-offs beating Inter-Roma 3-1 in both semi-finals, and then secured the play-off finals by beating Toronto Italia 2-0 and 1-0."

The final standings for the 1964 season:

CANADIAN EASTERN PROFESSIONAL SOCCER LEAGUE

	GP	W	T	L	GF	GA	PTS
Toronto City	24	14	6	4	67	41	34
Toronto Italia	24	13	5	6	58	34	31
Toronto Inter-Roma	24	11	4	9	53	47	26
Hamilton Steelers	24	6	4	14	45	70	16
Montreal Italia	24	5	3	16	32	62	13

Although the standard of Canadian football was good, it wasn't quite what Nigel had been used to in Division One of the English League. "The forwards were nowhere near as physical and the crowds that came out to watch were more on par with Scottish football attendances. Quite often whole stands would be completely empty - resembling practise matches back home." Having said that, Nigel had enjoyed his short 'summer break' in the Canadian province of Ontario immensely and he knew he would return. He just didn't know when.

At the close of the season, Nigel vacated his apartment at the Frontenac, making all the necessary arrangements for the return to England then boarding his transatlantic flight, bound for Heathrow. He was going back to the UK and the unknown. He had no contract from any football team waiting to be signed, although he did have one option, Plymouth Argyle. When Malcolm had left Toronto three months earlier to manage the 'Pilgrims,' he told Nigel to look him up when he came back to the UK. "There will always be a place for a goalkeeper of your ability in any of my sides Nigger," were Allison's last words to Nigel in Toronto.

Years later, Tony Book told Nigel he had followed Allison to Plymouth Argyle when he came back to the UK, though it hadn't been without complications. "I was advised by Malcolm to tell Plymouth that I was younger than I actually was, or they wouldn't have coughed up the fee of £1,500 to Bath City for my registration! I had already turned thirty by the time I came back to England and had never played League football. Non-League and Canadian football were my only achievements. When I handed my birth certificate to the Plymouth secretary, it had been folded in to quarters so many times in the past by my mother that it had holed slightly where it had creased. You couldn't make out properly the last digit in the year of my birth. I just told them I was born in 1936, not 1934, and with them thinking I was only 28, I was lucky enough to get away with it."

Nigel said, "Tony didn't realise just how good a footballer he really was. He saw himself as a bricklayer first and foremost and a part-time player at best. Later on, when he found out Manchester City were interested in taking him from Argyle, he said that he would be well out of his depth. I told him, 'don't be daft! You go up there and you will do fine.' He did just that."

"I looked up to Nigel," Tony explained. "In fact, all the lads who came out to Canada did. He had been an 'experienced pro' at the top of his game for quite a few seasons now. He had recently won Cup Finals with Aston Villa and had helped them get straight back up after dropping into the Second Division, Nigel was a big man, even by goalkeepers' standards, but he was very agile for his size, 'top drawer.' He also knew a lot about the game. Playing in front of Nigel made you feel comfortable and confident and I am sure that he played a part in making me become a better footballer. When I left Canada and went to Plymouth to join up with Allison, I didn't know he was only going to be there for just a year. I stayed put for another season at Home Park and then Malcolm contacted me again. This time, he had gone to a club, not as a manager, but to be Joe Mercer's right-hand man, so to speak, at Manchester City and he wanted me up there. They were a massive club and I just didn't know if I could cope with Division One. It was a big step for me to take. It was Nigel, as much as Malcolm that convinced me I should make the move up to Maine Road. They had watched me first-hand playing in Canada for Toronto against all different nationalities. There were Brazilians, Argentineans and loads of Italians over there. Me and Nigel got picked to play in a one-off game for an all Canadian XI against an International Italian XI."

Tony went on to make nearly two-hundred and fifty appearances for Manchester City's first team, many as captain. He won three trophies in his playing career, going on to manage the club to League Cup Final success in 1976 against Newcastle United. In fact, he made history by becoming the first person to win the League Cup as a player and as a manager.

Not bad at all for a 'brickie'!

CHAPTER SIXTEEN

AND FINALLY - A POSH BOY

"When I got back from Toronto, I landed at Heathrow. It was only when I was waiting to collect my suitcase, I thought, 'I don't really fancy Plymouth.' I didn't know the area and, apart from Malcolm Allison, I didn't know anybody else. So I made my way back to South Wales. When my Villa contract ended I'd left Wolverhampton and Wales is where I settled. I set up a home for myself in a bungalow at Dunvent, on the outskirts of Swansea. It's not far from the Gower Peninsular, it's a beautiful area."

"About a week or so after I came back to the UK, I got word that Reading and Peterborough United were interested in signing me. I had no club holding my registration and I was tempted to go with Peterborough. They offered me £600 to sign on with them. They'd just got into the Football League, and were promoted in their first season and then finished in the top ten of the Third Division for the next three seasons. Their manager was Gordon Clark and he had plans for his team. Willie Duff was the goalkeeper and he'd lost his form and couldn't get it back. He let in fifteen goals in their first seven fixtures. The deputy was, Tony Read, so Tony was put in the first team, he didn't impress the manager enough to give him a longer run, so the boss let it be known they would get someone in from outside the club. There were some decent players there that Peterborough had managed to pull in. I decided I wanted to be part of it, so I was given a contract until the following April."

Nigel was familiar with quite a few of the squad at his newest club. Two former Villa teammates were at London Road, Vic Crowe and Derek Dougan; the 'Doog' had joined Peterborough at the start of the previous season and had instantly acquired cult status throughout the London Road following, by banging in twenty-one. Nigel also knew fellow goalkeeper Willie Duff. Duff had also signed for the 'Posh' the season before and missed just four games, although he had recently been dropped from the first eleven. Willie had been the unfortunate 'keeper in the Second Division clash between Aston Villa and Charlton Athletic at Villa Park, when Villa ran riot, hitting eleven goals. Duff had gone off, as he dislocated a finger trying to stop goal number six. Another former teammate of Nigel's at Peterborough was ex-Wolves wing-half, Eddie Clamp. Nigel was also acquainted with forward Peter Deakin, who had recently signed from Bolton Wanderers. Nigel had come up against the striker when Villa had played the 'Trotters.' Before Nigel was in place at London Road, 'Posh' had played Tony Read in goal. He had shipped nine goals over the two games subsequently being dropped.

Nigel was given his debut at Kenilworth Road. He hoped that Dougan would emulate his performance of the previous week, when he had snatched a hat-trick at home to Mansfield Town. Dougan didn't deliver that day, 'Posh' settling for a 1-1 draw against Luton Town. Peterborough were sitting mid-table at that time. Two days later Nigel made his home debut when Brentford were the visitors to London Road. A healthy crowd of 13,311, boosted by approximately 3,000 more than expected for the fixture, witnessed Peterborough topple the Division's leaders 3-1. Nigel started the next two fixtures, which both ended in defeats.

Peter McNamee was out for the Kenilworth Road fixture, but was back in the side at London Road for Nigel's home debut and remembered it as something special. "Everyone in the dressing room was aware of Nigel's presence; a few of the lads were in awe of him. This was a player who had played at the top and had won Cup Finals. When we went out onto the pitch it was a different atmosphere, the feeling in the ground had changed slightly. I don't know how much of it was down to Nigel, or the fact we were playing the League leaders, but it was different. I can only liken it to a team in the Championship having David Beckham play for them. We got a world-class striker from the

Villa last year in Big Derek Dougan and now we had a world-class 'keeper."

Nigel was absent for an away game at Scunthorpe United, and youngster Brian Robinson was 'blooded' in goal. 'Posh' won 3-2, Brian retaining his place for the 2-2 draw at home to Port Vale. This, however, was a disappointing result, as Vale were hovering just above the drop zone.

When Walsall's 'Saddlers,' came visiting, Nigel was back in goal. He played his part in a 3-1 victory which saw striker Peter Deakin continue his fine form in front of goal scoring for the third game on the spin. "After playing top-flight football, there was a huge difference. The crosses coming over were easy to collect and the forwards didn't seem too interested in coming at me, trying to charge me into the net. It was a piece of cake!"

Vicarage Road came next with Peterborough looking to pick up more points on their travels - they had managed only one win in eight away fixtures, including five defeats. They played well against a well-disciplined Watford side earning a hard fought point finishing at 1-1.

When Peterborough faced Reading, it was a second-half Keith Smith brace that saw the 'Biscuitmen' off 2-1 at London Road. The half-time team talk by the manager had the desired result, the 'Posh' overturning their interval deficit. In the next home game, the fans were hoping for much of the same, but Peterborough went in trailing at the interval 1-0 to Workington. The 'Reds' from Cumbria hadn't read the script and duly came out in the second-half and put three more past the hapless 'Posh,' who failed to find the net. "Gordon Clark went mad after the whistle, absolutely mad. The guy was passionate, no mistake. This was Peterborough's biggest home defeat of the season. They only lost one more game at London Road all season, against Bristol City who were a very organised outfit under Fred Ford."

When Peterborough went to Boothferry Park, they came

away with a comfortable 2-0 win over Hull City. Peter McNamee and Dennis Shiels, who was standing in for Dougan, scored the vital goals and gave the 'Posh' boys a morale boost ahead of their coming FA Cup tie. Lowly Western Division side, Salisbury City, stood in the way of Peterborough's progressing further than last season, when Watford had put them out of the Cup, after a replay.

Peterborough managed to negotiate this potential 'banana skin' game without too much anxiety. Vic Crowe settled the home crowd's nerves scoring his first goal for the club. Former teammate Dougan, also bagged a goal and put the home side ahead 2-1 at the break. Salisbury were a spent force early in the second-half and the gulf in League placings between the sides became more obvious as the match wore on. The 'Doog' helped himself to a hat-trick claiming the match ball, while Peter Deakin weighed in with his sixth for the season. The hosts were good value for their 5-1 win.

Peterborough were then set to face Bristol City at Ashton Gate. A good game was on the cards in the West Country – the 'Robins' were the Division's highest scorers at that point having hit forty-nine goals. 'Posh' weren't so far behind them, having found the net forty-four times; so it was a game that the fans anticipated as guaranteeing goals. Nigel was powerless to stop City adding two second-half goals to the one they had netted in the first-half and 'Posh' went down 3-1.

Peterborough's lowest gate of the season so far, watched the clash with Queens Park Rangers. Only 8,337 braved the cold to witness the home side run riot. Outside-right Ron Barnes opened the scoring and Dougan added another to make it his tenth for the campaign. Then Deakin and McNamee each helped themselves to a double in Peterborough's 6-1 demolition of Rangers.

The following week, Queens Park Rangers held the home

advantage, when they faced their 'nemesis' Peterborough in the Second Round of the FA Cup. The 'Posh' surrendered an interval lead, but were grateful to take Rangers back to London Road for a replay following that 3-3 draw at Loftus Road.

The gate of 15,289 for the QPR Cup tie replay was almost double the number for the League match played only eleven days before - the magic of the Cup! With two more goals from Peter Deakin, who had managed to score in both of 'Posh's' previous Cup ties, the home side progressed, 2-1, to the third round where they had hoped to land one of the big clubs. The draw was unkind, in that sense, and they had to settle for an away tie to Chesterfield, in January.

Nigel was still playing in the team and produced clean sheets in both the next two League fixtures; at home to Exeter in a dull 0-0 draw and away at Bournemouth & Boscombe Athletic, claiming their fourth away win in the League, 1-0, courtesy of a Deakin goal.

Nigel's penultimate appearance in the Peterborough jersey came in the Boxing Day clash with Barnsley at London Road. He signed off in front of the home fans, playing his part in a convincing 4-1 victory.

And finally to Oakwell, the 'Tykes' little ground in South Yorkshire. It would witness the curtain fall on one of the country's finest post-war goalkeepers' careers. Nigel Sims and his glorious English football career came to a premature end, unknowingly, with a 3-2 defeat on December 28th 1964.

CHAPTER SEVENTEEN

THE FINAL CURTAIN

Nigel spent some time thinking about his next move and, by 1967, he decided to leave the UK and emigrate to Canada. "I loved the way of life during my short time in Toronto and, as I had nothing to keep me here, I thought I would try my hand back over there. When I returned to Canada, I knew that football wasn't going to be my only source of income. I'd landed a good job at Upper Canada College, teaching the students Physical Education. It was a private boarding school, very exclusive. It was a beautiful place." As well as being the PT or PE instructor, Nigel turned out on a regular basis for the College Staff Soccer side that played in a local League. One of the matches was against another local team who had in its side expat 'Brummie,' Norman Crandles. Norman recounts the day; "I was fortunate to play against Nigel Sims in my early days, shortly after emigrating. That would be around 1967 or '68. I was playing for a local team in a League that included the staff of Upper Canada College, Canada's premier private (public) school. Nigel was the PE teacher and he turned out for them. Needless to say I wasn't only overjoyed, but overawed, at the proposition of playing against the man who, a scant decade earlier had been instrumental in us (Aston Villa) winning the FA Cup. You can imagine how high I was when we eventually took the field. I can't remember much about the game except to say that we were awarded a penalty and I was (you guessed it!) our designated taker. It really was a dilemma for me because, of my deference towards those heroes; even though I had a modest degree of notoriety myself as a singer!" He was actually a lead singer with a well-known 'Brum' band in the early/mid '60s, known as Lee Stevens and the Satellites. Norman was Lee Stevens. "My band was well-known in 'Brum' and I came to know a few of the Villa players, notably 'Doog,' Bobby T, Harry Burrows and most of 'Mercer's Minors' as well as Jimmy MacEwan - who was certainly no minor. I was tongue-tied, and still am around my Villa heroes.

As it happens I scored, but not without some misgivings.

After the game we mingled with the other team and I sat with Nigel on the grass for some time talking about all things Villa. He was clearly very shyly pleased to be so publicly adulated, particularly as I was able to give him chapter and verse on the final, and probably knew more about the Villa than he did! In any event, it was one of the most exciting times I've ever had playing the game and he was such a gentleman spending so much time with me. Nigel was extremely modest and completely 'un-glorified,' which to me was a huge deal, given his standing in the game at the time of his retirement."

When Nigel returned to Canada he initially signed for local side Toronto Falcons. "They had only been formed that year (1967). They played their home games at the Varsity Stadium, just as we did when I played with Toronto City three or four years before. City had played in the Eastern Canadian Professional League, but The Falcons played their football in the National Professional Soccer League (NPSL). I only got to play two matches for them. The fourth 'keeper on the Falcons' books was Jamaican, Gauntlett Rowe - a classic name for a goalkeeper that was!" Nigel chuckled. "Like me Gauntlett only made two appearances; Bill Brown, the former 'Spurs' and Scotland custodian, shared the position with Juan Benegas, a Spaniard, who had played in his home country, mostly with Deportivo La Coruna." In the two games Nigel played, he let in three goals but pulled off an amazing twenty-seven saves. The Falcons finished the season in fourth position in the Western Division, failing to qualify for the play-offs.

Western Division

	G	W	T	L	GF	GA	P
Oakland Clippers	32	19	5	8	64	34	185
St Louis Stars	32	14	7	11	54	57	156
Chicago Spurs	32	10	11	11	50	55	142
Toronto Falcons	**32**	**10**	**5**	**17**	**59**	**70**	**127**
Los Angeles Toros	32	7	10	15	42	61	114

"There were some financial irregularities at the club and it was rumoured that they were close to going out of business. I didn't bother hanging around to find out. I signed on with Toronto Italia."

The Falcons started their second season in the newly-formed North American Soccer League (NASL), but folded at the end of the '68 campaign.

During Nigel's second spell in Canada, he was joined over there by former Villa teammates, Vic Crowe and Phil Woosnam, who represented Atlanta Chiefs, and Harry Burrows who was now playing his football back home for Stoke City, and turning out for the Cleveland Stokers.

In contrast to Nigel's short time with Toronto Falcons, he played in the majority of games for Italia. Not long before the season's conclusion, the team flew to Pennsylvania to face the 'Spartans.'

"While playing for Italia against Philadelphia, their centre-forward, Peter Short an English lad from Liverpool, came at me with such force. It was my own fault, I didn't move out of the way quickly enough and my leg was caught on the side of my shin about five inches below my knee. Like a fool I stayed on the pitch and kept taking all the goal kicks during the game. As the game, went on it got more painful. I should have had more sense and gone off, or got the full-back to take the kicks at the very least; but in them days you never let on when you were hurting, you just didn't do it. By the end of the game my foot was hanging limp, I had ruptured and torn quite a few ligaments and I was in bloody agony. My club's medics assisted me off the pitch and a coach drove us from the stadium to the team hotel. I sat up all night in a chair in my room, I couldn't move at all. I had no sleep. It was a long, long night and the pain was excruciating. The following day we took a flight to Chicago. I was in a terrible state and it was that bad that, on landing, they had an ambulance take me directly to the hospital. The nurses met me at the door and I was taken straight in. A doctor had a look at the damage, saying he would soon sort it. They put this big old-fashioned hood thing, like a tent, over my legs. There were strong light bulbs under the hood that were incredibly hot - the idea was that the heat would help with the leg injury - but it didn't feel right. I called a nurse and told her what they were doing was wrong. She said that she wouldn't tell me how to play soccer and that it was just my imagination that the treatment wasn't working and then went away. Later in the afternoon, when the doctor called on his rounds, he saw the state of my leg and 'all hell broke loose.' He demanded to know why the nurses hadn't been checking on me regularly, and if they had, why had he not been informed? They removed the lights quickly enough now. They had caused the blood to clot, so then I was thinking, bloody hell, I'll end up losing the leg. They rubbed and tried manipulating the leg to stimulate blood flow and then injected me with the biggest bloody needle I had ever seen, something to supposedly thin the blood. It didn't work the way they wanted it to and this fluid they put into me set solid. Now I needed surgery, but I wanted it done by someone I could trust, so it was put off to be done when I got back to Toronto."

"Later that evening I was laid in bed, thinking I was still asleep having some sort of nightmare. People were running around screaming and shouting, 'It's coming this way, it's coming this way!' Then I could hear, 'It's lifting, it's lifting." (Nigel was drifting in and out of sleep). "The next day I was taken by taxi to the airport and I realised that I hadn't been dreaming at all. A tornado had hit Chicago and come directly over the hospital. Everywhere was flattened, the place was just decimated, and the houses to the one side of the hospital had been razed to the ground. By some miracle, the tornado had lifted clear and the hospital was totally untouched, but it had come back down on the other side and wreaked absolute havoc. Honestly it was just terrible to see. Past the estate and the hotel I'd stayed in the night before with the rest of the team, it was all flattened and half the hotel had gone. You couldn't believe it."

"When we got back to Toronto, I was taken to see the soccer club's surgeon. 'What a mess Nigel, what the hell have you done?' he said. It took him ages to remove all the hardened fluid and dead cells and then clean the wound. He said I was in worse shape than roadkill!"

"There was a specialist surgeon based in Toronto and he'd trained at St Guy's Hospital in London. Unfortunately he was up in the Northern Province at that time. Every year he went round all the Native Canadian people reservations to check on their well-being and all that. He was away for six weeks, but he saw me straight away as soon as he got back. He looked at my leg and the extent of the damage was so bad I was given two options. I could live the rest of my days with a shoe with a raised sole; or, the alternative was to have this highly complex muscle and tendon graft surgery. I wasn't too keen on the shoe idea, so I chose the operation. My entire shinbone had to be scraped, leaving the front lower leg totally devoid of muscle. I could have had more surgery to build it up, but was told it was a very high-risk procedure with only a very miniscule success rate. The new tissue might not have taken and survived as there was hardly anything for it to knit onto. That would have meant having a lot of muscle and skin taken from different parts of my body and as there might have been no point, I didn't have it."

Nigel's shinbone nowadays is almost razor sharp. Fans like me look up to and envy these famous former footballers - men who won Cup Final medals, played for our favourite teams. Yet we have no idea of the pain and suffering that a lot of these players experience on a daily basis. Even to this day, Nigel has to keep going to hospital to have his shin periodically scraped and cleaned as it weeps continually. Swimming is something he has to do regularly, to keep his leg active; towelling himself dry after swimming requires extreme care, dabbing himself, as rubbing causes bleeding.

This was the ultimate injury that put paid to his glittering football career. "I must have done something right; I played for two massive Midlands clubs, though I didn't get to play many for the first of them (Wolves). I was in the Villa Cup winning sides of '57 and '61. I won the 'Terrace Trophy', which was just as special to me, as you have to remember this was recognition from Villa's marvellous supporters. I loved them, still do! I loved my time at Aston Villa and felt privileged to pull on the jersey for them. I played lower down the Leagues at a very good, forward-looking outfit in the 'Posh' and I was also fortunate to play in Canada. I am very thankful for my lot. At different times in my career, Arsenal, Manchester United, Liverpool, Newcastle United, and some big Italian sides wanted me, including Juventus, who were keen to have me. Then there was also Nuneaton Borough, they were really keen, they wouldn't take no for an answer!"

Nigel's gloves and boots were finally hung up for the last time. The football career that little David Nigel Sims, growing up in a remote Derbyshire village had dreamt of, had run its course. Luckily for fans of the football world, but especially Wolves, Aston Villa, Peterborough and a trio of Toronto soccer teams, Nigel had lived his dream, and in doing so he was able to give countless thousands of supporters many happy 'football memories.'

CHAPTER EIGHTEEN

THE GREEN GREEN GRASS OF HOME

Nigel returned to the UK a month or so after having surgery and he knew that football was a thing of the past. Looking on the bright side though, he had both his legs and he could still walk, so he was grateful for that.

He came back to Swansea for a time before getting a call from an old friend, Fred Cooper. Fred was Chairman of at least five companies most of which were located in the Midlands area; Nigel was taken on as manager at one of Fred's woodworking factories. "I was there for a number of years, it was good work and I enjoyed it, but some personal issues meant that I had to give up my job and go back to Swansea."

Another friend of Nigel's was John a salesman for the Prudential Insurance Company; they met when Nigel had bought a policy with them. John pointed Nigel in the right direction and he became a salesman too but he was used to something a bit more 'hands on.' Although this work didn't suit him he stuck it out for a few years before returning to working with his hands, after all they'd never let him down before! Good old Fred Cooper came up trumps again with another job offer, this time it was in South America – Brazil - and what a tempting offer it was! Nigel, though, was reliant on regular hospital treatment; this was the 1970s and Brazil was not exactly a world leader in medical treatments, Nigel thought it was best to turn down the offer and stick with what he knew. "Fred was a wonderful bloke. When I was manager for him, he took the entire workforce to Benidorm one year and wouldn't let us pay for a thing. In fact, he did that more than once. When I told him I couldn't go to work for him abroad, he sent his secretary down to see me in Swansea. 'This is for you, off Fred', she said, handing me an envelope. Bloody hell, it was a cheque for £5,000. What a star bloke he was."

In the early 1980s, Nigel saw an advert – 'Woodworkers wanted.' He phoned up and it turned out to be Terry Carless who was an old acquaintance. Terry gave Nigel a job and, over the next few months, this master craftsman taught a willing student all he needed to know in order to go out and work for himself, as a carpenter.

Nigel bought a little van and with Terry supplying the timber from his factory in Telford, Nigel was up and running. 'Luxifit' was born. Nigel had settled in Swansea and there was plenty of work to be had. One of his earliest jobs was to supply and fit a pair of sliding door, bedroom wardrobes for a local born girl, Marjorie Gibby. During the war, Marjorie's father had been a Flight Lieutenant and after he became a prominent figure in the community working as the local bank manager. Nigel and Marjorie's path would cross a few times and, before too long, they were dating. Marjorie knew that Nigel had played 'a bit of football' before, as she had asked about the injuries to his legs. Then, a few weeks later, she was at home doing the housework with the radio playing in the background. Tommy Smith, the ex-Liverpool full-back was being interviewed and he was asked who had been an opponent that had stood out, and been difficult to beat. His reply was Nigel Sims the ex-Villa goalkeeper. Marjorie was astounded and couldn't wait to see him later that night and ask if he was the same Nigel Sims and of course, he was! It didn't make any difference to either of them whether he had been famous or not, and their romance flourished regardless. They married in Marjorie's home town of Swansea. "I remember the first time I saw for myself how special he had been in the past. It was when Aston Villa invited Nigel up to Birmingham. It was the last game of the season and the club were due to demolish the big stand behind the goal, straight after the match (Holte End's 'last stand' May 7th 1994.) As soon as we got out of the car there were fans just about everywhere. Everyone wanted to shake them big hands. Most were talking about 1957 and it seemed they all loved him, even the small children knew who he was! It was like when you see royalty on the TV. I have to admit, it was a very special day and I felt very proud of my husband."

When Aston Villa were drawn at home to Manchester United in the FA Cup Third Round, January 5th 2008, for the fourth time in only seven seasons, Nigel, his wife Marjorie and two other '57 Cup winners, Peter McParland and Jackie Sewell were the match guests of Aston Villa owner Mr Randolph Lerner. In the lounge during half-time, Nigel was told the Governor of the Bank of England was at the game. "Not likely," was Nigel's reply. Mervyn King who is the Governor, and happens to be an Aston Villa supporter overheard the conversation and introduced himself. During their chat it transpired that when Nigel played for the Villa, he lived in Wolverhampton and a very young Mervyn King, who was eight-years-old when Nigel signed for the Villa, lived directly across the street.

Nigel and Marjorie have been together now for 'far too many years to recall.' Both are settled and happy, living in Marjorie's hometown of Swansea. Marjorie comes from a large family and every Christmas they have a big get together with as many as sixty-five relatives attending.

Every year Nigel and his Marjorie take a holiday in Switzerland where Marjorie's daughter Debbie has lived for over twenty years. Her son Leighton lives local to Swansea; he and his wife Julie, have two sons, Dale and Adam.

Nigel has his work cut out - only the one grandson is a Villa fan - up to now!

CHAPTER NINETEEN

TESTIMONIES

Eric Houghton (Aston Villa manager, Sep '53-Nov '58)

Nigel Sims - the best in my time though Fred Biddlestone was good. Jimmy Dugdale and Nigel Sims were the best signings I made in my life! *Extracts taken from 'The Villa News & Record' 1990.*

Stan Crowther

Stan Crowther (Aston Villa)

"We were having a team meeting on the Friday before the Bristol City Cup tie (Fifth Round 1957) and Eric Houghton was reading it out. He came to John Atyeo (the Bristol centre-forward) and turning to Jimmy Dugdale he said. 'He'll never go down your left side'." During the game, Jimmy went towards him, Atyeo went past him, on the left, past Stan Lynn. Atyeo, hits this ball with his left foot, Simsy didn't see it. He went up for it but never got near it, and it was in the top corner. Nigel comes back down and looks at me as I'm getting back into the penalty box and says 'Stan.' I says, 'what Nige?' and he says 'no left foot?' Sometimes you'd get where there's so much tension in a match, then someone would say something to break it and everybody laughs. We were coming back on the train from Villa one day and he (Nigel) got a pack of cards out, it wasn't long before I was losing quite a lot of money so I opened the window and chucked the cards out. Nigel went mad. For a big man he could shift. He was a really big guy, I used to love him, and we used to have some great times! Stan and Nigel used to socialise, they used to frequent the Sir Tatton Sykes. End of!"

Peter McNamee

Peter McNamee (Peterborough United)

"Nigel was a larger than life character. A great fellow, and always fun to be with. He kept everyone laughing, and was so funny. We didn't know him that well, as he didn't live in the area, he travelled over from the Midlands. The funniest thing I can remember? We were up at Blackpool, training for a Cup tie, staying at the Norbreck Hotel. The manager Gordon Clark, he must have been fifty-three-years-old, we got him to race with Nigel. So they are bent down then, three, two, one and off they went. The manager was about twenty yards in front of him then flew up in the air - he'd pulled a muscle! Nigel said, 'I'm glad he's out the way' and we said, 'he was, he was well in front of you.' Nigel said, 'Look, I was giving him a twenty-yard start!'

"On an evening in Blackpool Nigel was sitting playing blackjack. The dealer gave him a card and looking at it he said, 'very happy'. We were all stood behind him and burst out laughing. He turns swearing and says 'she knows I have nothing now, cheers lads!'"

Harry Burrows (Aston Villa)

"Nigel had a great sense of humour. After regular training was finished he would say, 'come on let's do another twenty minutes.' I would line up eight or nine balls. As soon as I hit the first and Nigel was diving, he would shout 'next one,' stop the ball and jump up in one movement. He would just keep doing that, on and on. As quick as I could kick them, he would be down for them. For his size, his agility was marvellous. I played alongside Gordon Banks and I have to say Nigel was on par with him. After shooting, I might take some balls over to the wing and hit crosses for him. He always had trouble with his weight pre-season. He wore a plastic suit under his tracksuit and the weather in July and August was sometimes hot. Nigel would strip off in the dressing room and there would be a big pool of water round him! Extremely professional, it always showed in his games. There were lots of very good 'keepers around and he was up there with them. He was one of the best."

Harry's thoughts on Nigel's never being capped were due to the fact that the England team was chosen by a select committee and Villa didn't have a member on that board.

Harry recalled an incident where the Villa team were out doing a training run along canal towpaths. "Nigel was in his usual place, at the rear of the group. There was a bit of larking about and then next thing - Pat Saward and Nigel were both trying to pull themselves out of the canal!"

Malcolm Finlayson (Wolves)
"Nigel had moved to Aston Villa by the time I left Millwall for the Wolves, but he still lived in Wolverhampton and we would meet up socially, as we mixed with the same crowd. There was a mutual admiration for one another. I thought Nigel was a very good goalkeeper; in my own opinion, he was a better goalkeeper than either Bolton's Eddie Hopkinson, or Alan Hodgkinson of Sheffield United. Both played for England and Nigel never got a cap. Both were comparatively small chaps for 'keepers; small 'keepers are usually agile, throwing themselves all over the place, whereas Nigel and me would take a step to the side and catch the ball. They would be leaping all over the place

turning the ball round the post, making it look like a great save and the selectors were impressed with that kind of thing. There was a selection committee made up of directors from various football clubs, and they would always push for their own teams' players. This is how it was until Walter Winterbottom was appointed national team manager. Nigel actually, was a good goalkeeper, and we used to pull each other's legs because he and I had a similar build. We used to joke about playing at Villa Park and kicking the ball from one end of the pitch to the other, and that was a ball that was actually a 'real man's' football."

Jimmy MacEwan

Jimmy MacEwan (Aston Villa)
"When I first joined the Villa, Nigel was on loan at Arsenal, so I didn't get to meet him immediately. When he returned, the first thing he did was to come across and introduce himself. The other lads had told me how easy he was to get along with, and I took to Nigel straightaway. Watching him in training, he did things that should have been impossible for a big lad. I've seen many a wee fellow far less agile than 'Simsy.' Nigel won us a lot of games and in big or important matches he would make some wisecrack remarks to relax his defence."

Gordon Lee

Gordon Lee (Aston Villa)

"The one thing that always sticks in my mind was when we were training and doing shooting practise. Nigel always had this saying, and it will stay with my all my life. He would say, 'You wouldn't beat my missus from there.' He was a big handsome bugger, Nigel. Goalkeeping for me isn't about saving penalties and diving here and there, they are expected to do that anyway. It's about having an aura and Nigel had that in abundance. When Nigel caught the ball and stood there, you turned round and you'd think, ok, well there's no way they are going to score today; because he had a presence, an aura, this charisma about him. He was a big confident lad without being big-headed. There weren't many of them about. I think that's why he was what he was. If the conditions were bad and you were under the cosh, a cross would come in and he would come and just stand there and it was as if he went from 6'ft 5" to 7ft 5. That was possibly the most important thing a goalkeeper had to have and they either have it or they haven't got it. But Nigel had this. Goalkeeping is about giving confidence to the defenders playing in front of you. Nigel oozed confidence into us by the way he stood there. When you play for a big club - and in them days, when we were at Villa, they were a big club and expectations were very, very high. That was an extra demand on the goalkeeper and one mistake would lead to a goal. You needed good mental strength to overcome that and in fairness he (Nigel) did. Remember, there were a lot of goalkeepers who came to Villa and left quickly. He is a very modest guy and a good friend."

Tony Book (Toronto City)

"I was a Non-League player and went over, meeting up with all the lads in Canada. Nigel was one of them. After a few weeks of playing in the team, Nigel was the one who went and spoke to Malcolm Allison saying he thought I could do it at top level. The pair of them were impressed with how I had coped. Malcolm left Plymouth for Manchester City after twelve months. I stayed down at Argyle for another season and when Man City came in for me, it was Nigel I asked 'should I take the chance?' I knew he had played at the top level and I wanted to know if I'd be able to cope. Nigel said 'Tony you'll have no problem with it.' Nigel was one of the lads I looked up to because he was an experienced pro at top level. He was a big lad, but very agile for a big person. He was top drawer."

Alan O'Neill (Aston Villa)

"I was stopping at Bobby Thomson's house in Wolverhampton over Christmas. Nigel lived straight over the road. When we got up on Christmas morning, we were sat having a cuppa and a chat and someone says, 'where's the little fella?' Bobby's little lad. 'Oh, he's gone across to Nigel's.' Just then, here comes Nigel walking back over the road holding the lad's hand. The doorbell goes and he says, 'here take this 'un, he's been bouncing these billiard balls all over my new piano.'

"When I first went to the Villa and we trained at the 'Hercules,' we would take shots at Nigel. He had this habit of catching the ball putting it under his arm and looking at an imaginary watch. He was taking the 'mickey' saying 'stop wasting my time and give me something to save.' He was a lovely man, a big gentle giant of a man. During my time at the club, he was suffering from a bad thigh injury. I got on really well with Nige! "Whenever we were standing around listening in training sessions, he always used to stand with his hands clasped and would be twiddling his thumbs."

Peter Deakin

Peter Deakin (Peterborough United)
"Nigel was only here for a short time, when we were embarking on that Cup run that took us to the Sixth Round. I remember clearly Nigel's first game for us at Luton. He was absolutely outstanding, especially in the first-half. He stopped everything. Gordon Clark signed him as an understudy for Willie Duff. Willie was the regular goalkeeper; Nigel made an enormous contribution to the team, even though he wasn't playing every game. He was so popular that when we went up to Blackpool to Norbreck Castle for special training during our Cup run, the players specifically requested that Nigel also go along. Nigel was included, he was such an ebullient kind of character, very funny and upbeat and good for morale. He was a nice guy and such an influence for good. Even though he was only there for a short time, I can summarise that he was a good type of a guy, very easy to get on with, an asset to any group. Of course 'Clarky' saw that, because 'Clarky,' he, was very good on the man management side. So including Nigel in them trips proved to be a successful move."

Ron Wylie (Aston Villa)

"Our son Nigel, who is forty-six, now, was named after Nigel Sims, because we had so much admiration for him, he was such a great goalkeeper. Nigel was an absolute legend. He was extremely professional and he was also so laid back in games, he put everyone at ease. I remember one game in particular. We were under terrific pressure, a corner came across. He came out shouting it was his ball, we stayed out of the way as he jumped up and caught it, making it look very easy. Before he even landed on the floor, he would look towards his wrist and shout 'Hey Ron its quarter past three,' I thought, 'you bloody big head, that's absolutely brilliant.' He was a funny man."

Alan Deakin (Aston Villa)

"I got on well with Nigel, he's a lovely bloke. You know, I can't remember seeing a bigger 'keeper than Nigel during all the time I played and I don't think I ever saw one that was much better agility wise either. There was an abundance of good goalkeepers about in the years when Nige played at the Villa. Some really good ones and he was up there with the best of them. Peter Bonetti of Chelsea was a very quick-footed goalkeeper and had lightning reflexes; he was probably the closest to Nigel for ability."

Nigel Stevenson (Executive Hospitality Steward Villa Park)

"I would love to have my name recorded in the roll of honour, not only because I have been a Villa fan since the day I was born, but more significantly, my dear old dad, William 'Billy' Stevenson named me Nigel - after Nigel Sims. My dad was born in Aston in 1916 within the sounds of the Trinity Church bells, so naturally he was a Villa fan too from the day he was born. He eventually met my mother, Doris Swain. They married and went on to have six children, all of whom were named by my mother, except me. I was born in, 1958, my mother was going to name me Paul, but my dad put his foot down and told her adamantly that it was his turn. He declared that I should be named 'Nigel' after the great Nigel Sims. Dad spent the rest of his life proudly telling everyone, that his youngest son was named after one of the greatest keepers that ever played for the Villa. Three years ago, whilst on North Stand matchday duty, I saw two distinguished gentleman walking towards the reception. I instantly recognised Peter McParland, but I was not too sure about the other. Asking a colleague, I was told that the other gent was a Villa goalkeeping legend from the 1950s. I approached and said 'Mr Sims?' To which he gently smiled and replied 'yes.' Well you could have knocked me down with a feather, 'I've been waiting fifty years to meet you, I'm your namesake!' We both laughed; I showed him my Villa name badge and told him the story of how my dad had named me Nigel after him and how lucky I was to meet him at last. I will never forget meeting Nigel and am so proud to have been named after him, such a great Villa player, a legend and a true gentleman."

Nigel Sims' Career Statistics

Wolverhampton Wanderers (total 39)

Appearances	League	FA Cup	League Cup	Clean Sheets
1948/49	4	0	0	1
1949/50	1	0	0	1
1950/51	0	0	0	0
1951/52	4	0	0	0
1952/53	13	0	0	4
1953/54	8	1	0	1
1954/55	3	0	0	0
1955/56	5	0	0	0

Aston Villa (total 310)

Appearances	League	FA Cup	League Cup	Clean Sheets
1955/56	9	0	0	6
1956/57	38	9	0	14
1957/58*	41	3	0	6
1958/59	41	6	0	7
1959/60	39	5	0	15
1960/61	30	2	9	6
1961/62	28	4	1	9
1962/63	13	0	2	4
1963/64	25	2	2	9

Arsenal (loan) (total 2)

Appearances		
1958/59	2 Friendlies:	Italy/Switzerland Tour

Peterborough United (total 19)

Appearances	League	FA Cup	League Cup	Clean Sheets
1964/65	16	3	0	4

ECPSL**

Toronto City (total 28)

Appearances	League	Play-offs		Clean Sheets
1964***	24	4		10

NPSL.****

Toronto Falcons (total 2)

Appearances	League	Play-offs		Clean Sheets
1967	2	0	-	0

Toronto Italia

Appearances	League	Play-offs		Clean Sheets
1967	17	0	-	6

Nigel Sims played a total of 310 first team appearances for Aston Villa.

This figure doesn't include friendlies, testimonials or Aston Villa 'public matches.

* 1957/58 Nigel made an additional first team appearance; playing in the 1957 Charity Shield at Old Trafford against Manchester United

** ECPSL Eastern Canadian Professional Soccer League.

*** 1964 Nigel played four matches in the play-offs, two in the semis and two in the final.

**** NPSL National Professional Soccer League.

Bibliography

Books

Aston Villa, The Complete Record Rob Bishop & Frank Holt

The Villa News & Record, Official Journal of the Aston Villa Football Club Limited

Aston Villa, The First 100 Years Peter Morris

Aston Villa, A History From 1905 Historic Newspapers

The Official History of the F.A. Cup Byron Butler

The Complete Encyclopaedia of Aston Villa Football Club Tony Matthews

Villa in the blood Bernard Bale

Who's Who of Aston Villa Tony Matthews

English Football League & F.A. Premier League Tables 1888 – 2009 Michael Robinson

Sky Sports Football Yearbook 2008 – 2009 Glenda Rollin & Jack Rollin

Peterborough United - The Official History of The Posh Andy Groom & Mick Robinson

Maine Man, The Tony Book Story Tony Book & David Clayton

IN SAFE HANDS: NIGEL SIMS' FOOTBALL MEMORIES

Big Mal, The High Life and Hard Times Of Malcolm Allison, Football Legend David Tossell

Jackie Sewell Keith Dixon

The Gerry Hitchens Story, From Mine to Milan Simon Goodyear

The Real Bobby Dazzler, The Bobby Thomson Story Simon Goodyear

Aston Villa, Head to Head Peter Waring

Going for Goal, My Life in Football by Aston Villa's flying Irishmen Peter McParland

Heroes and Villains, Aston Villa Fanzine Dave Woodhall

Peterborough United Official Programme

Websites

The Rise and Fall of the Eastern Canadian Professional Soccer League taken from www.soccerreportextra.com

Aston Villa news taken from www.astonvilla-mad.co.uk

North American Soccer League Rosters www.nasljerseys.com

Nigel Sims information www.wolvesheroes.com

Peterborough United Database www.uptheposh.com

Aston Villa History John Lerwill www.lerwill-life.org.uk

Heroes and Villains www.heroesandvillains.co.uk

Peterborough United statistics www.peterborough-mad.co.uk

Every effort has been made to fulfil requirements with regard to reproducing copyright material. The authors and publisher will be glad to rectify any omissions at the earliest opportunity.

Aston Villa, The complete Record, was the sole source for attendances regarding Aston Villa matches!
Some of the information in this publication is hearsay from interviews conducted with former footballers.

Roll of Honour

Presentation Copies

Nigel & Marjorie Sims
Aston Villa F.C.
Mayor of Peterborough
Neil Alderson
Norman Hood, Cartoons
Kyle 'ABZ' Abbott
Andy~Vaughan Media
Aston Villa archives

Ron & Shirley Wylie
Jimmy MacEwan
Stan Crowther
Gordon Lee
Alan O'Neill
Charlie Aitken
Harry Burrows
Alan Deakin

Colin J. Abbott
Nigel Simons
Mark Alan Clarey
Jon Farrelly
Dave Clarke
Richard J. Bourne
Alan Goodall
Tom Goodall
Martin 'aka Mozza' Moss
Andy 'Turnstile' Ullah
Nigel Stevenson
Peter Lane ~
~Peterborough United Historian~
& wife Sandee
Keith Morris
Andy Greenhalgh
Marc Taylor
Tracy & Hayley
Laura Brett

Neville Evans
Malcolm Finlayson
Peter Deakin
Robert R. Abbott
Peter Donohoe
Pam Bridgewater
Dave Bridgewater
Sue & Mick Tilt
In Memoriam Johnny Dixon
In Memoriam Jimmy Dugdale
In Memoriam Gerry Hitchens
In Memoriam Vic Crowe
In Memoriam John Sleeuwenhoek
Alan Gee
Karl Court
Andrew Owen
Nigel Paskin
Andrea Paskin
David Hodges (Southam)
Clive Waldron
Graham Boulton
Robin David Wilkes
Robert Gough (Daventry)
John Lerwill
Brian C. Seadon
Simon Goodyear
Roger Wilks
Peter McNamee
Billy Dumbrell
Steve Knott

Alan Goulding, Newport,Shropshire~
Ex Groundstaff under Bert Bond,~
First Season 1962-63
Bryan Shaw
Peter J. Ross (Belbroughton)
Paul A. Weston
Phil Fellows
Nigel Stanton
Peter Stanisstreet
Will Hughes~Forever Villa
Richard Leach
David B. Collins~
Dad & Grandad~
Love from David, Gill Sammi & Gary
Eddie Ratcliffe
K J. Knowles
Dave Woodhall
Chris Bickers
Sammy Mackie
Nigel was my first Villa 'keeper~
and probably the best~
Keith Johnstone
Ade Nevett
John Knight
Terry Knight
Mike d'Abreu
Mark Jones
David John Coley
Johnny Walker
Barrie Rhodes
Mark Goodwin
Kenneth Moore
Brian Foster

IN SAFE HANDS: NIGEL SIMS' FOOTBALL MEMORIES

Roy Cresswell
Christopher John Turner
Wendy Jordan
Paul Haynes
Graydon Daley
Bradley Lyndon
Tilly Janie Marjorie

251

abz
publications